MW01109386

The $3.5 Trillion Advantage

The $3.5 Trillion Advantage

A Marketer's Guide to Revenue Growth In Today's America

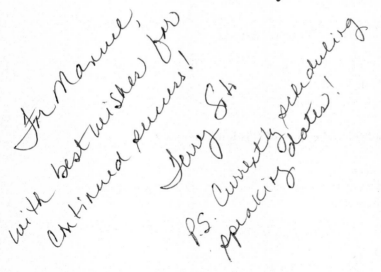

Terry J. Soto

Copyright © 2019 by Terry J. Soto.

Library of Congress Control Number: 2018913771
ISBN: Hardcover   978-1-9845-6716-1
                     Softcover   978-1-9845-6715-4
                     eBook   978-1-9845-6714-7

All rights reserved. No part of this book may be reproduced or
transmitted in any form or by any means, electronic or mechanical,
including photocopying, recording, or by any information storage and
retrieval system, without permission in writing from the copyright
owner.

Print information available on the last page.

Rev. date: 12/13/2018

To order additional copies of this book, contact:
Xlibris
1-888-795-4274
www.Xlibris.com
Orders@Xlibris.com
785506

Contents

To my father and friend, Cesar M. Soto, who sadly passed while I was writing. His courage to venture to a new country, work ethic, sacrifices, generosity, and never-ending encouragement will forever inspire my work to improve my clients', my family's, my colleagues', and my community's well-being.

Foreword

The United States of today offers businesses the ability to accelerate sales growth by implementing their strategies among multicultural consumers—a population that greatly expands the domestic core markets on which firms are currently focused. This book is a compelling reframing of multicultural markets as the next horizon of revenue growth. It helps companies ready themselves to serve this market and capture this growth with a long view while growing the value of their businesses.

It also deals with some tough questions: Why are many companies myopic and apprehensive when it comes to targeting multicultural consumers? Why are so many multicultural efforts ad hoc, devoid of strategic alignment and limited in scope, investment, and continuity?

Investor groups, board members, and CEOs with an eye on revenue growth should read this book. They are tasked to think about how to relevantly expand their companies' strategies to grow sales in new markets. While this typically implies international expansion, the U.S. multicultural market presents an opportunity for strategy expansion and revenue growth domestically.

Think about it. With all the uncertainties that exist in global markets, multicultural consumers here on our own soil give American companies the unique ability to leverage their strategic strengths and assets to grow revenue in a new and lucrative marketplace with a fraction of the resources it takes to do so on foreign soil. Leaders would be remiss not to ready their organizations to benefit from this expanding population.

An eye toward intelligent expansion coupled with the day-to-day work it takes to achieve success into the future is what leadership is about. Vision matters, as the parable of the three stonemasons illustrates.

A traveler comes across three stonemasons, each carving a block of stone at a construction site. The traveler asks what they are doing.

"I'm carefully carving a line in this block of stone," the first stonemason says.

"I'm carving this stone so that it matches the one beside it to make an archway," says the second thoughtfully.

And the traveler asks the third, "What are *you* doing?"

"I'm building a cathedral!" says the third with excitement.

The third mason had an all-encompassing view of his enterprise. It takes foresight and an eye on the horizon to understand that investment in everyday tasks will lead to something much grander—that our *task* today may be to carve stone but our *purpose* is to build a cathedral.

This straightforward book recognizes and highlights simple truths that I've observed in my own work on the corporate side—that diverse customers are often high value and sometimes more profitable than "traditional" core customer targets and that a diverse labor force and growing a multicultural customer base can go a long way in strengthening the bottom line of any business. But as with any growth endeavor, companies must be strategic, and they must be patient as they work intently to win over the various multicultural populations; it doesn't happen overnight.

This is not a book about how to make the most culturally competent and award-winning television commercial or brochure. Soto would tell us that dominance in a new market requires much more than marketing. This book is about the professional business practices required to integrate a new market or consumer group into an existing business process. Visionary leadership will be required. It's time to get to work.

Russell A. Bennett
Retired, Vice President, UnitedHealthcare
Opportunity Strategy and Development and
Latino Health Solutions

Introduction

I've been observing and advising senior executives in large U.S., Latin American, and European Fortune 1000 companies on how to gain dominance in the U.S. Hispanic market since the late 1980s. Many of the companies I've advised have made tremendous headway and enjoy dominant Hispanic market positions in their respective industries. Several were already dominant when they sought my advice but were seeking to maximize their position by assuring their competitive strategy implementation remained relevant to consumers and competitive in their industries. A few companies veered off course, and their occasional marketing efforts were insufficient to put them on the path to market dominance. All the while, many more companies continue to sit idle and do little to position their companies to dominate the multicultural market.

Why is this important? We live in exciting times, replete with opportunity. The economy and consumer confidence are strong, and people are spending lots of money. And multicultural consumers are well on their way to spending $3.5 trillion this year—a sizable share of the country's buying power. Considering these spending dynamics, what company wouldn't want to expand its business strategies into this market and do so in a way that enables it to dominate multicultural spending in its industry?

I believe the multicultural market has been largely underappreciated by corporate America for the last three decades, and it remains so even as it is upending companies' views of the average consumer. This is a dangerous position to be in because it keeps many companies from capturing a powerful revenue source.

There are several reasons my work and this book are so important to me. To begin with, I am an immigrant. My parents brought me to the United States when I was a child, and their arduous work, sacrifice, and encouragement created the well-educated and professional woman I am today. My parents worked tirelessly to build a thriving business; they owned three homes, bought new cars every two to three years, took yearly vacations, and loved shopping. Not a day goes by when I don't feel immense pride in my parents' success. And my story repeats itself in millions of households in America.

I know it's hard to appreciate the aspirations, the work ethic, the upward mobility, and the spending power of a community that may be very different and about which one might know little about. Therefore, one of my greatest satisfactions in my three-decade career has been helping my clients see and appreciate multicultural consumers, and Hispanics in particular, as human beings, not only as an interesting, hardworking, diverse population but also as powerful consumers who spend a substantial portion of their income on the products and services sold by American and multinational companies in this country but may not be buying from your company—yet.

An amazing thing happens when companies become familiar with and start appreciating these consumers in the context of how they do business. These customers feel appreciated, and they, in turn, reward the companies by opening their wallets. And they recommend their brands to friends and family. This two-way appreciation creates a symbiotic relationship that translates into powerful market value.

Advising companies on how to expand and implement their strategies with appreciation and relevance has been the focus of my work for almost thirty years, and this book helps explain some key principles. The goals for this book are threefold. First, it helps companies understand that America's demographics have changed and will continue to change dramatically. Even more important, this change brings tremendous economic benefits for American companies that align their organizations to appreciate these consumers. Second, it helps companies see that the current methods of targeting multicultural markets is not working. It's not working for the companies for which the economic benefit remains under optimized, it's not working for the executives assigned to manage multicultural work, it's not working for the agencies to which this responsibility is assigned, and it's not working for multicultural consumers who must travel through irrelevant purchase paths. Third, this book shares the strategic thinking required to help companies reframe this marketplace, its spending, and the panacea it represents to companies on a constant search for new sources of revenue.

This book offers a critical business proposition for the investment community, board members, CEOs, and senior leaders to appreciate this consumer market as the powerful future revenue stream it represents today and into the future. The book also speaks to defining how this appreciation of multicultural consumers can develop within their organization and the work required to ensure that every aspect of the organization is aligned advantageously to win over these consumers. Companies needn't reinvent the wheel, nor do they need to change their strategies or business models.

I've often pondered the causes for the lag I see among companies that haven't expanded their strategies or haven't organized to implement them in U.S. multicultural markets. It can't be the fear of the unfamiliar because Fortune 1000 companies successfully expand and implement their strategies in new markets in Asia, Europe, and Latin America all the time, and they invest tremendous resources to do so because they know that's what it takes to be successful in these markets. It can't be a lack understanding or knowledge about multicultural markets or their spending power and propensity to buy across a range of products and services because there are dozens of books on the subject. White papers and reports from reputable think tanks abound. Industry sales data exists. And an enormous number of market-research publication companies publish reports incessantly on these very consumers. It can't be xenophobia or anti-immigrant sentiment, even considering the current political climate, because most companies are smart enough to see through this, and they seldom allow political rhetoric to get in the way of their business success.

So what must companies do to succeed? I propose the following:
1. Those responsible for strategy formulation and implementation must broaden their views of today's consumer and develop a present-day and futuristic view of America's consumer market and the impact on their companies' current and future revenue growth.

2. Companies must realize there is no need to change their strategies and business models to target multicultural consumers. Most companies' strategies and business models are relevant to multicultural consumers. More importantly, they are proven domestically and, in some cases, globally. This minimizes the often-inherent risk of implementing new strategies in new markets. The focus instead needs to be on relevant implementation that demonstrates an understanding of and appreciation for multicultural consumers' needs and wants.

3. As multicultural markets have grown exponentially in the last three decades, companies' implementation must also evolve. In the early 1980s, the multicultural market was small. Efforts to attract them were minimal, ad hoc, and tactical—mostly focused on advertising. Today, by and large, they remain at this elementary level. However, to succeed among today's enormous, fast-growing, and multifaceted multicultural consumers, companies must evolve and move toward greater integration of implementation efforts and move away from ad hoc, intermittent, and underfunded approaches. The market has grown too big, too sophisticated, and too economically powerful. Efforts to attract and retain it must reflect this change.

4. Multicultural targeting efforts must become integrated into the company's way of doing business. It must become part of objectives, goals, implementation, budgets, communication, training, and accountability metrics to be effective. There is no such thing as a general market and a multicultural strategy. Companies have one strategy that they must implement relevantly in the many markets they target, including multicultural markets.

5. Companies must prepare and build cultural intelligence as a core competency among their work force so they more easily understand, relate to and ultimately grow to appreciate consumers who may be different from themselves. Today's middle manager, C-suite, and boards have not taken steps to develop their employees' cultural competency, and this contributes to managers' tendency to delegate the responsibility for multicultural efforts to junior people or outside the organization rather than integrating within their

planning and implementation responsibilities. It isn't enough to become a more diverse organization. Non multicultural employees must develop their cultural intelligence to avoid hesitancy and passing the multicultural ball around like a hot potato.

In Chapter 5, I talk about the 1999 book *Alchemy of Growth* by Mehrdad Baghai, Stephen Coley, and David White, longtime McKinsey consultants. Their Three Horizons Framework, a time-honored planning structure used by many successful businesses, makes sense for companies looking for new revenue streams with future growth potential. It proposes that companies must always keep an eye on the horizon for new and expanding revenue-growth opportunities and organize to benefit from them as the environment changes.

Multicultural markets should be seen and pursued as a future revenue stream because they no doubt represent the next significant revenue source for American companies, especially as a sizable portion of the non multicultural population ages and dies. Companies cannot afford to keep avoiding these markets or to keep testing the waters. The waters have been tested by their competitors for years, and these competitors have been happily swimming in an ocean of lagging companies' lost revenue. It's time to jump into the deep end with conviction and start swimming toward multicultural market appreciation and dominance.

Acknowledgments

I thought I knew exactly what I wanted to write, but easily, I went off course with all the disruptive political rhetoric and its nationwide impact on marketers' perceptions of multicultural markets in the country. Fortunately, some very wise and supportive friends and colleagues gave me much-needed reality checks.

I'm very grateful to the following: Russell A. Bennett, former vice president of opportunity strategy and development and Latino solutions for the UnitedHealthcare Group; Mark Stockdale, former vice president of multicultural marketing for T-Mobile; Johanna Marolf, former director of the Latino Market at H&R Block; Bryan Garcia, strategic planner extraordinaire at Conill Advertising; Gloria Tostado, former multicultural marketing executive at Verizon Wireless, BMO Harris Bank, and Circuit City; Angel Colón, senior director of diversity, multicultural development, and supplier diversity at Kroger Co; Lisa Kranc, former senior vice president of marketing for AutoZone; and Luis Nieto, retired president of ConAgra Consumer Products—all of whom gave so generously their time to provide invaluable input and for their willingness to openly share their experiences in multicultural markets and help ground this book in the real world of strategic thinking and implementation.

My sincere appreciation also goes to my well-respected colleagues—Carlos Santiago, president and chief strategist at the Santiago Solutions Group; Cesar Melgoza, founder and CEO of Geoscape; Gilbert Davila, president and CEO of Davila Multicultural Insights; and David Wellisch, cofounder and CEO of Collage Group—all of whom made time in their busy schedules to talk at length about my ideas for the book and shared openly (without breaking confidentiality) about their own observations and experiences, their philosophies, and their outlooks. Their feedback on my thinking was invaluable and helped shape the direction and content of the book.

I thank Peter Francese—a widely recognized demographics and consumer behavior expert, founder and president of *American Demographics* magazine, and advisor and principal of the New England Consulting Group—for taking the time to speak with me and for crunching some great census data for me. And I thank Jorge Daboub and Roberto Ruiz at Univision for making their treasure trove of industry presentations and data available to me. It saved me so much time.

A special thank-you goes to Nina Taylor, my editor, who patiently and ruthlessly chopped and wordsmithed my manuscript until it made sense, not to mention the hand-holding and encouragement as I approached my deadlines.

And finally, a big thank-you goes to the team at Xlibris for making the publishing of this book such a pleasant and smooth experience.

Chapter 1

The Big Shift

Two demographic transformations are in play in the United States right now: a record share of the population is going gray, and the population is rapidly becoming majority non-white. According to Paul Taylor of the Pew Research Center, "each of these shifts would, by itself, be the defining demographic story of its era. The fact that both are unfolding simultaneously has generated big generation gaps that will put stress on our politics, families, pocketbooks, entitlement programs and social cohesion."

According to Nielsen, multicultural consumers are the fastest growing segment of the U.S. population. The U.S. multicultural population is over 120 million strong and represents 38 percent of the country's population. It is projected to be the majority population by 2044. In 2015, Nielsen reported this multicultural population was growing by 2.3 million people per year, 191,932 people every month, 6,310 people every day, and 263 people every hour.

The multicultural population is young. The U.S. Census projects that by 2020, 50 percent of the population under eighteen years of age and 46 percent of adults aged eighteen to forty-nine will be multicultural, while 65 percent of adults aged forty-five to sixty-five and 76 percent of adults sixty-five and older will be non-Hispanic white. This ethnicity–age contrast is depicted in Figure 1.1.

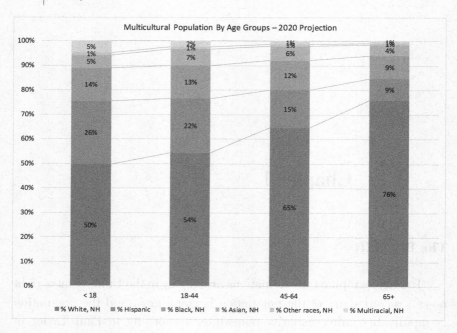

Source: 2015, U.S. Census Bureau (2020 Estimates)

Figure 1.1. Multicultural population by age groups (2020 projection).

The compound effect of a large and growing multicultural market that is both young and in prime childbearing years and a declining non-Hispanic white population because of aging and lower birth rates will result in a non-Hispanic white population size decline from 62 percent in 2015 to 44 percent by 2060.

The Cultural Evolution

This demographic shift has created two divides—a generational divide created by generational differences between multicultural and non-Hispanic white populations and the unavoidable cultural differences given the fastest growing proportions of multicultural Gen Z, Y, and X populations in history compared to the nearly homogenous racial and cultural profiles of boomer and senior generations.

Multicultural populations are upsetting outdated assumptions that they would assimilate and blend in. Instead, multicultural populations have adapted to an appreciation for and identification with the duality of their culture, and they are exerting unprecedented influence on the attitudes and consumption habits of non-Hispanic white consumers, resulting in tremendous revenue growth opportunities for American businesses across most industries.

Multicultural icons in politics, music, sports, film, science, literature, fashion, and food have been shifting mainstream U.S. culture and preferences for the better part of the past three decades. Who would have thought salsa would outsell ketchup and tortillas would outsell bread because of the affinity for Hispanic foods among non-Hispanic white and other Americans?

This cultural shift among non-Hispanic white populations has been most pronounced among Gen Z, Y, and X populations. Multiculturalism is so interwoven into the day-to-day world of these generations, they can't imagine life any other way. At the same time, multicultural Gen Z, Y, and X populations embrace and expect a multicultural upbringing where a cultural give-and-take across cultures is a way of life.

Overcoming the Generational Hurdle

Commenting on a recent article on strategic relevance I had contributed to *retailwire.com*, Dan Stanek, EVP of Big Red Rooster, said, "One of the underlying reasons companies have been slow to stay current with the changing marketplace is that innovation is more difficult when leaders are much older than the target market and they do not understand how they think."

Is he right? It's a thorny question to ponder but one that must be asked. Is the older age skew of America's primarily non-Hispanic white business leaders affecting their ability to stay current with changing demographics and culturally driven preferences? Could it be that the current generational and cultural divide impacts older generations' ability to see the value in attracting top-line growth in the multicultural marketplace? Is it strange and uncomfortable for older leaders to pursue unfamiliar markets versus those they know well? Successful innovation requires the older generation of leaders to broaden their understanding of the country's current population and to develop a level of cultural intelligence to enable them to adapt to the differences.

The New Face of America

The demographic face of America has been constantly changing since tens of thousands of immigrants started arriving from Europe in the 1600s. But that was just the beginning. Let's look at how immigration has evolved in the twentieth and twenty-first centuries among Hispanic, Asian, and African American populations.

Hispanic Market Demographic Outlook

The most recent immigration waves of the 1940s, 1960s, and 1990s were led by people coming from Latin America but predominantly from Mexico because of the country's shared border with the United States. The domestic labor vacuum caused by World War II, the agriculture labor shortage in the sixties, and the economic expansion that created significant labor demands in the eighties and nineties all contributed to the ever-growing demand for and recruitment of Mexican immigrants to fill the labor gaps.

Since Hispanics started arriving in the United States, the Hispanic population has now numbered 58.9 million and increased 2.1 percent between 2016 and 2017 according to the U.S. Census. The Hispanic population made up 18.1 percent of the nation's total population in 2017, primarily because of natural increase (the difference between births and deaths). Between 2016 and 2017, Hispanics represented 51 percent of total population growth and 66 percent growth since 2000. By comparison, non-Hispanic whites represented 9 percent and 16 percent of total population growth during this same period, respectively.

All projections indicate this fast-paced growth will maintain pace such that by 2040, Hispanics are projected to represent 24 percent of the total population and 29 percent by 2060. Even taking the slowing immigration and a reduction of birth rates since the 2008 recession, Hispanics are still expected to account for 65 percent of the nation's population growth over the next forty-five years, meaning the U.S. Hispanic population will more than double to a population of more than 119 million by 2060.

Asian Market Demographic Outlook

Chinese Asians started arriving in the United States during the latter half of the nineteenth century because of the California Gold Rush. Beginning in the early 1960s and throughout the remainder of the Cold War, America welcomed Asians from communist countries. Asian immigration gained significant momentum in the 1990s during the country's ten years of economic boom and again in the 2000s during the United States' postindustrial Information Age to fill America's high-skilled labor gaps in the technology sector.

The Asian population has grown the fastest via immigration since 2000. As immigration from Latin America has declined in recent years, China and India have been outpacing Mexico in immigration flow into the United States. According to the U.S. Census, The Asian population increased 3.1 percent to 22.2 million between 2016 and 2017 and represented 6.1 percent of the U.S. population. Asians were the fastest growing racial group in the nation. Their increase is primarily due to net migration, and the census projects the U.S. Asian population will reach 25.7 million by 2019. By 2055, Asian immigrants are projected to make up a greater share of all immigrants, becoming the largest foreign-born group in the United States, according to Pew Research Center estimates.

African American Market Demographic Outlook

Between the seventeenth and nineteenth centuries, hundreds of thousands of Europeans arrived in the United States to build a new life and a new country. Many of those who had arrived were sent from the prisons as indentured servants to fill the need for labor. However, this labor force was not enough. To meet growing labor demands, the first African slaves were brought to Jamestown, Virginia, in 1619 to help with the lucrative tobacco, rice, and indigo crops. Slavery in the colonies in the seventeenth and eighteenth centuries helped build the economic foundations of the United States. In the mid-nineteenth century, slavery was abolished, freeing over four million slaves. It is estimated that six to seven million African slaves were brought to America during this time, but many died because of disease and mistreatment.

The Selig Center reports that the African American population grew by 1.2 percent to 46.8 million between 2016 and 2017. From 2017 to 2022, the African American population is projected to grow by 5.9 percent, exceeding the 4.3 percent growth projected for the total U.S. population. The African American population also grew faster that the non-Hispanic white population. From 2000 to 2017, the population grew by 21.7 percent compared to 9.4 percent for the non-Hispanic white population and 15.8 percent for the total population. African Americans of all races are expected to grow to 74.5 million by 2060 and are expected to represent 17.9 percent of the country's population.

Today African Americans are of West or Central African and European descent, and some also have Native American ancestry. Additionally, a 2014 Pew Research Center survey of Latino adults shows that 24 percent of U.S. Hispanics self-identify as Afro-Latino, Afro-Caribbean, or of African descent with roots in Latin America.

Non-Hispanic White American Market Demographic Outlook

Most of the United States' non-Hispanic white population ancestry reflects its European immigrant history. These ancestries are predominantly German, British, Scandinavian, Italian, and Irish. There are those who claim their ancestry is "American" because their families have been in the country for generations and they no longer identify with their ancestral lands.

According to the Pew Research Center, there is also a trend toward mixed-race marriages where non-Hispanic whites are marrying Hispanics, Asians, African Americans, Arabs, and others, causing the mixed-race population to grow three times faster than the rest of the total population and now represent almost 6.9 percent of the population in America.

The U.S. Census indicates that non-Hispanic whites were the only population group to experience a decline between 2016 and 2017 (-0.02

percent). This was also the only group that reported more deaths than births from July 2016 to July 2017. The census projects that the non-Hispanic white population will shrink over the coming decades, from 199 million in 2020 to 179 million in 2060. By 2050, the non-Hispanic white population is expected to represent less than half the U.S. population, while the rest of the population will be a combination of non-European ethnicities.

Non-Hispanic whites will still be the single largest ethnic group in America, but together, ethnic minorities will represent a "majority minority" population. By 2060, the non-Hispanic white population will decline to 44 percent of Americans, and 35 percent of people aged sixty-five and over will be non-Hispanic white, while 64 percent of younger population segments will be multicultural. This demographic shift in the U.S. population is seismic and demands an aggressive shift in businesses' perspective to adapt to and benefit from this demographic transformation.

It's important to recognize that this transformation is in the country's DNA and is reflective of a more globalized, multiracial, and multicultural population like those present in countries around the world. Understandably, this transformation causes unease among non-Hispanic white populations—especially boomers and seniors—because for some, the country's population shift may suggest a cultural change, a loss of position and a loss of control. However, these sentiments are not new; they have resurfaced during every wave of immigration this nation has ever experienced.

Growing Economic Clout

With $3.5 *trillion* in buying power, the multicultural population is already driving growth for dozens of product and service categories produced by American and multinational companies that recognized the direction of the country's demographics early on. These companies took steps to expand their strategies and align their implementation in ways that are relevant to multicultural markets, where many now enjoy a competitive advantage.

As the size and economic clout of the multicultural population continues to grow, U.S. companies have a tremendous opportunity to benefit from the incremental revenue potential multicultural populations represent. Indeed, leaders stand to benefit from reframing the multicultural market as a viable revenue growth opportunity by broadening their view beyond the status quo.

This will require stepping out of comfort zones and the familiar and embracing new and up-to-date thinking to embrace new markets. The path to successfully gaining a position of advantage in this market is increasing relevance. Being relevant requires gaining comfort and familiarity with new cultures. Importantly, it requires developing not only an understanding but also an appreciation of multicultural populations as people who have similar needs for products and services, albeit with some differences driven by their cultural backgrounds that need to be understood and accommodated.

Mark Stockdale, who led T-Mobile's Hispanic market success for many years, believes it's not so complicated. He says, "It's about embracing the cultural nuances rather than thinking there are diametrically opposed differences. It's a cultural manifestation—not a matter of focusing on opposites." Smart leaders will apply this understanding and appreciation to ensure their organizations expand their business strategies to multicultural consumers in relevant ways. This is the only way to ensure positive customer experiences that will keep these consumers coming back and, hopefully, delighting them to the point that they become champions for companies' brands.

You might ask, "How is this relevance manifested?" It starts with understanding the values, beliefs, attitudes, and behaviors related to a product or service category and integrating this knowledge in innovation work, communication approaches, and strategy delivery in general, including sourcing, distribution channels, merchandising, operations, human resources, and infrastructure.

Capitalizing on a new market opportunity is not easy. It can be disruptive, especially when one first attempts to understand them. But if we think of the big successes in business of late, disruptors play a big part, and those companies that lead the disruption always gain the position of advantage.

Shifting Economics

The Selig Center's report entitled "The Multicultural Economy" projected that the nation's total buying power was $14.6 trillion in 2017 and that it would rise to $17.4 trillion in 2022. The multicultural population's buying power of $3.5 trillion represents almost one quarter of all spending power and is comparable to the GDP of Germany, the world's fourth largest economy. Multicultural buying power is expected to grow by 34 percent to $4.7 trillion by 2022. This tremendous buying power signals extraordinary opportunities to expand business strategies to new economically viable markets within the country's borders.

Hispanic Market Economic Outlook

According to "The Multicultural Economy," Hispanics controlled $1.5 trillion in buying power in 2017, making its buying power larger than all but twelve world economies (2017 GDP measured in U.S. dollars); it is smaller than the GDP of South Korea and larger than the GDP of Australia.

Hispanic buying power accounted for 10.3 percent of all U.S. buying power and reflected a 203 percent increase from the year 2000—far greater than the 87 percent projected increase for the non-Hispanic white population and the 97 percent increase for the total U.S. population. Hispanic buying power is expected to reach $1.9 trillion by 2022 and will represent just over 11 percent of total U.S. buying power. However, in many of the markets where Hispanics are now a large and growing proportions of the population, the strength of their buying power is palpable.

As Table 1.1 shows, Mexicans, the largest of the Hispanic population groups, account for $854 billion in buying power or 57 percent of Hispanic buying power. The remaining 43 percent is controlled by Puerto Ricans, Central Americans, South Americans, and Cubans.

Table 1.1:
Hispanic Buying Power (2017)

Total Hispanics	Mexicans	Puerto Ricans	Central Americans	South Americans	Cubans
$1.5 trillion	$854 billion	$158 billion	$133 billion	$129 billion	$79 billion
10.3% of total U.S. buying power	57.1% of Hispanic buying power	10.6% of Hispanic buying power	8.9% of Hispanic buying power	8.7% of Hispanic buying power	6.7% of Hispanic buying power

Source: The Selig Center, "The Multicultural Economy," 2017

Buying-power differences can also be seen by state. More established geographies where Hispanics go back multiple generations control the largest proportions of buying power. Table 1.2 shows the proportions for the top ten states as of 2017. In rank order, they were New Mexico, Texas, California, Florida, Arizona, Nevada, Colorado, New Jersey, New York, and Illinois.

Table 1.2:
Hispanic Buying Power Share (2017)

States	Hispanic Buying Power Share
New Mexico	33.7%
Texas	22.8%
California	19.7%
Florida	17.8%
Arizona	17.2%
Nevada	16.1%
Colorado	11%
New Jersey	11%
New York	10.6%
Illinois	9.1%

Source: The Selig Center, The Multicultural Economy," 2017

Large population size, a significant proportion of U.S.-born Hispanics, high birth rates, younger age skews, robust labor-force participation, increasing education, and strong entrepreneurial spirit all contribute to Hispanics' sizable and growing buying power. For example, the number of Hispanic-owned firms increased by 46 percent from 2007 to 2012, fifteen times faster than the 3 percent increase in the number of all U.S. firms. While college degrees among Hispanics might seem to lag other groups at 16.4 percent, census analysts point to the high proportion of significantly less-educated foreign-born Hispanics as a factor that weighs down this number. The gap is closing; in 2014, 35 percent of college-age Hispanics compared to 33 percent of college-age African Americans, 42 percent of college-age non-Hispanic whites, and 64 percent of college-age Asians were enrolled in college.

Collectively, the impact of all these factors can be seen in Hispanics' increasing affluence. Household earnings of $75,000 or more doubled to 26 percent between 2000 and 2016.

Asian Market Economic Outlook

According to the Selig Center's 2017 "The Multicultural Economy" report, Asian buying power in the United States reached $986 billion in 2017, a 257 percent gain from 2000. This gain exceeded the projected 87 percent gain for the non-Hispanic white population, 97 percent gain for the total U.S. population, 108 percent gain for African Americans, and the 203 percent gain for Hispanics.

The Asian population buying power was larger than the entire economies of all but sixteen countries in the world—slightly smaller than the GDP of Mexico and slightly larger than the GDP of Turkey.

Asian buying power is expected to increase to $1.3 trillion by 2022. Table 1.3 shows that Asian Indians control $266 billion in buying power or 27 percent of Asian buying power, the largest proportion of any other Asian population. Another 54 percent is controlled by Chinese, Filipino, Korean, and Vietnamese populations, and the residual 19 percent is controlled by the rest of the U.S. Asian population.

Table 1.3:
Asian Buying Power (2017)

Total Asians	Asian Indian	Chinese	Filipino	Korean	Vietnamese
$986 billion	$266 billion	$231 billion	$147 billion	$81 billion	$71 billion
6.8% of total U.S. buying power	27% of Asian buying power	23.4% of Asian buying power	14.92% of Asian buying power	8.2% of Asian buying power	7.2% of Asian buying power

Source: The Selig Center, "The Multicultural Economy," 2017

Asians are the country's most affluent population, with a household median income of $74,829—39 percent greater than the national median income of $53,657. Like Hispanic buying power, Asian buying power is concentrated in geographies with large concentrations of Asian populations. In some cases, these are markets where Asians have lived for generations. Table 1.4 shows the six states with the largest shares of Asian buying power in 2017. In rank order, they are Hawaii, California, New Jersey, Washington, Nevada, and New York.

Table 1.4:
Asian Buying Power Share (2017)

States	Asian Buying Power Share
Hawaii	45.2%
California	16.4%
New Jersey	11.6%
Washington	9.9%
Nevada	9.2%
New York	8.5%

Source: The Selig Center, "The Multicultural Economy," 2017

Job growth, strong immigration trends, urban concentrations, younger age skews, high-level corporate positions, and strong entrepreneurship all contribute to Asians' significant buying power. Asians are also much better educated than the average American and hold many top-level jobs in management, professional, and scientific specialties. Fifty-nine percent of Asians over age twenty-five have a bachelor's degree or higher compared to 33.7 percent of non-Hispanic whites, and the number of Asian-owned small businesses increased by 24 percent from 2007 to 2012—eight times faster than the 3 percent increase in the number of all U.S. small businesses.

African American Market Economic Outlook

According to the Selig Center, African American buying power was estimated at $1.3 trillion in 2017, representing a 108 percent increase from 2000 and an 8.7 percent share of national buying power. The 108 percent increase between 2000 and 2017 outstrips the 87 percent rise in white buying power and the 97 percent increase in total U.S. household buying power.

According to the World Bank, African Americans' buying power in 2016 made it the fifteenth largest economy in the world in terms of GDP. African American buying power is expected to grow to $1.5 trillion by 2022.

The Selig Center report points out that unlike the Hispanic and Asian populations, the African American consumer population is spread out, making it an attractive segment in many states. In 2017, the five largest African American markets accounted for 40 percent of African American buying power, and the five states with the largest total consumer markets accounted for 39 percent of total buying power. Similarly, the ten largest black markets account for 62 percent of the African American market, and the ten largest total consumer markets account for 56 percent of total buying power.

Table 1.5 shows the ten states with the largest share of African American buying power in rank order. Located in mostly the South, these states include Mississippi, the District of Columbia, Maryland, Georgia,

Louisiana, Alabama, South Carolina, Delaware, North Carolina, and Virginia.

Table 1.5:
African American Buying Power Share (2017)

States	African American Buying Power Share
Mississippi	24.7%
District of Columbia	24.2%
Maryland	23.3%
Georgia	22.8%
Louisiana	20.2%
Alabama	18.1%
South Carolina	18.0%
Delaware	16.7%
North Carolina	15.2%
Virginia	13.3%

Source: The Selig Center, "The Multicultural Economy," 2017

According to the Selig Center report, more African Americans are starting and expanding their own businesses, with the number of black-owned firms growing to 34 percent between 2007 and 2012—more than eleven times the 3 percent gain in the number of all U.S. firms. African Americans also continue to become more highly educated, increasingly making them ideal candidates for higher salary positions. Although African Americans attend college at lower rates than non-Hispanic white (33 percent) and Asian (56 percent) populations, college attendance increased by 109 percent between 1990 and 2016 to 23 percent.

It's important to note that African American households earning $75,000 or more per year are growing faster than among non-Hispanic whites in all income groups above $60,000. The largest income increase for African American households was among households making over $200,000, which grew by 138 percent compared to 74 percent among the total U.S. population.

The Lifetime Value Advantage

One of the strongest characteristics among multicultural consumers is their youth. As the non-Hispanic white population ages, multicultural consumers remain five to fifteen years younger. The economic significance of this age difference to U.S. companies is dramatic because it means that the lifetime economic value of multicultural consumers is much greater than for their older non-Hispanic white counterparts.

During an interview with Mark Stockdale, he said, "Customer lifetime value is a common measure marketers embrace to value what a potential target consumer represents to their business. The objective is to identify those consumers who can spend the most on your brand during their lifetime as a consumer group." Stockdale adds that "thinking of consumers' life stage, a basic principle in brand management, is helpful when identifying consumer groups with the greatest lifetime value potential."

The relative youth of multicultural consumers places them squarely in life stages where consumption for most consumer products and services categories is strongest. Tweens, teens, young adults, young families, and families with (multiple) children have much higher spending potential on main consumer goods categories than older boomers, senior empty nesters, or retired households for instance. Older boomers' and seniors' retirement life stage place them in decreasing income brackets, which impacts their spending power as they age. Figure 1.2 clearly shows how consumer spending starts declining after age fifty-four, dropping to an average of $38,691 per year among adults seventy-five and older from a peak of $71,166 among forty-five- to fifty-four-year-olds.

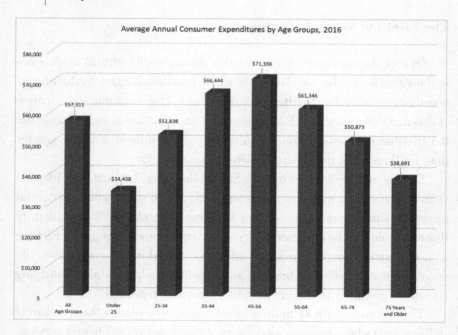

Source: Consumer Expenditure Survey, U.S. Bureau of Labor Statistics, August 2017

Figure 1.2. Average annual consumer expenditure by age groups (2016).

Figure 1.3 shows declining spending for several consumer products and services categories—including groceries, restaurants, housing, apparel, and transportation—among sixty-five-to seventy-four-year-olds while spending on health care, entertainment, and insurance increases.

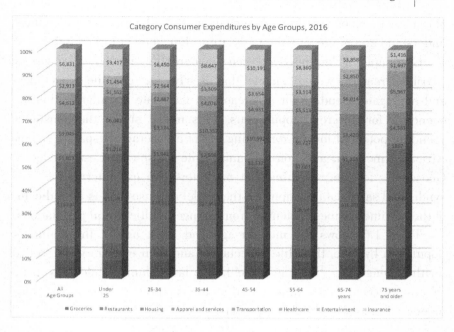

Source: Consumer Expenditure Survey, U.S. Bureau of Labor Statistics, August 2017

Figure 1.3. Category consumer expenditures by age groups (2016). With a median age of twenty-nine for Hispanics compared to forty-three for non-Hispanic white consumers, the Hispanic population is 61 percent more likely than the non-Hispanic white population to be planning their first home purchase, 60 percent more likely to be planning to marry, and 34 percent more likely to have a first or second child within the next twelve months. These life events come with considerable spending activity on related products and services. To achieve the organic growth many industries are looking for, they will need to win over younger multicultural populations as customers.

According to a Pew Research Center analysis, about one-third (17.9 million) of the nation's Hispanic population is younger than eighteen, and about a quarter (14.6 million) of all Hispanics are millennials (ages eighteen to thirty-three)—58 percent in total. Comparatively, only four in ten non-Hispanic whites are millennials or younger (39 percent). Overall, one in five millennials is Hispanic, and between 2016 and 2026, Hispanics are expected to account for 100 percent of millennial population growth.

Marketers intent on capturing and engaging the millennial generation must understand and appreciate the multicultural makeup of millennials.

Geoscape, a Miami-based geo-demographic analysis division of Claritas, created a valuable model that uses average age, life expectancy, and aggregate spending for a category to calculate cumulative lifetime spending for different populations. This model shows the consumer spending potential for the remaining life of an average Hispanic, Asian, African American, and non-Hispanic white household. Cesar Melgoza, Geoscape's founder, explains that marketers can use internal sales or syndicated sales data as inputs to the model and use this as an indicator of the lifetime business potential from younger multicultural populations.

Table 1.6 shows the median age and adult age of the country's population by race, their life expectancy, and their span in years to live (or their remaining "lifetime value"). The last column would reflect the lifetime projected sales value based on a company's average yearly sales among these four population segments.

Table 1.6:
Multicultural Population Lifetime Value

	Median Age	Life Expectancy	Span in Years	Lifetime Projected Sales Value
Hispanic	27.3	82.4	44.8	
Asian	36.8	83.8	40.7	
Black	33.8	77.7	33.8	
Non-Hispanic White	44.4	82.6	30.7	

Source: Geoscape, AMDS 2017 Executive Summary Report

Several cultural, demographic, and behavioral variables will affect the cumulative lifetime spending of a household. When these variables are used as inputs in the Geoscape model, the results, as shown in Figure 1.4, show that over their lifetime, the average Asian household will spend $2.65 million or $1 million more than the average non-Hispanic white household, while the average Hispanic household will spend $2.26 million or $625 thousand more.

As these two populations continue to grow rapidly, their aggregate spending will continue to grow in ways that companies cannot afford to undervalue as a driving force in revenue growth now and in the future. This makes it critical for companies to expand their sales and marketing strategies to these consumer markets by shifting focus and the necessary resources to do so.

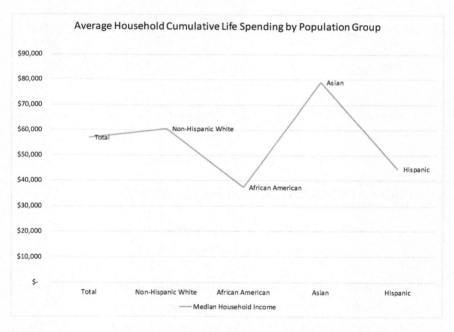

Source: Geoscape, AMDS 2017 Executive Summary Report

Figure 1.4. Average household cumulative
life spending by population group.

Figure 1.5 illustrates the projected food-at-home (grocery sales) lifetime value through 2060 using cumulative household spending data from the Bureau of Labor Statistics' Consumer Expenditure Survey. It is clear to see the significant lifetime value of groceries sales among Hispanics and Asians as compared to African American and non-Hispanic white consumer households.

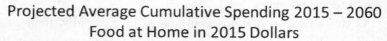

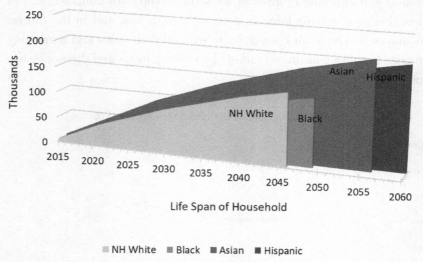

Source: Geoscape, AMDS 2017 Executive Summary Report

Figure 1.5. Lifetime value of groceries based
on population groups (2015–2060).

The United States continues to transform demographically and culturally. Explosive population growth, significantly younger profiles, and powerful spending power increasingly position multicultural consumers as the most powerful revenue-generating force of the twenty-first century. This is exciting news for American businesses looking for new revenue streams. Successfully capturing this new revenue flow requires a broader consumer perspective, an understanding and appreciation for new consumer markets, and the ability to organize and mobilize the organization to expand and deliver business strategies relevantly.

Chapter 2

Creating Economic Value

International expansion is increasingly important as more and more companies struggle to achieve meaningful growth and increased market value in the United States. For this reason, interest in expanding strategies to the BRIC nations (Brazil, Russia, India, and China) to grow revenue and value for shareholders is always increasing. Yet expanding into international markets can be complex, time consuming, and expensive and break even, and profits are usually off on the horizon. The good news is that international expansion isn't the only path to revenue growth and value creation.

As Chapter 1 revealed, the U.S. multicultural population is an economic powerhouse, with the GDPs of African American and Hispanic populations each being larger than all but thirteen countries in the world and Asian buying power being larger than the GDP of all but sixteen countries. Moreover, the multicultural population in the United States has a higher per capita buying power than consumers in any of the four BRIC countries. Moreover, as growth slows in BRIC countries and companies grow increasingly disillusioned with Europe and Japan also because of slower growth, some companies are turning their focus back to the United States. They are recalibrating their investment domestically and responding to increased competition. They are also very tuned into multicultural population trends as an important reason to see the United States as an emerging market—domestically.

In 2013, Procter & Gamble Co. slowed its expansion into "category-country combinations" in emerging markets to focus on its top forty most profitable existing ones—which are disproportionately in the United States. Unilever, Coca-Cola, and Reckitt Benckiser were also increasingly looking to the United States to compensate for international sales and volume declines. In Q4 2017, P&G's vice chairman and chief financial officer, Jon Moeller, communicated to investors and analysts during their fourth-quarter earnings report that "developing market growth slowed from over 6 percent last fiscal to about 5 percent this year."

In talks with L'Oréal investors and analysts in 2013, Frédéric Rozé, managing director of North America for L'Oréal, said, "The U.S. market will remain very dynamic structurally because the population is growing—twenty-seven million more inhabitants in ten years. The percentage of Hispanics, Asians, and African Americans keeps growing. They contribute to winning elections, but more importantly, they're over consumers of beauty products. That's one reason L'Oréal has moved up to number five from number twenty-five among top media spenders in the United States." In the first half of 2018, L'Oréal's CEO, Jean-Paul Agon, reported that as of Q2 2018, the profitability of L'Oréal's consumer products increased from 19.8 percent to 20.8 percent.

The magnitude of the multicultural population's demographic and economic power is as transformational as the postwar baby boom, and their purchasing power is set to have a profound long-term economic impact on the U.S. economy and American businesses.

Expenditure Growth

Based on the Consumer Expenditure Survey data published by the Bureau of Labor Statistics, Collage Group, a strategy and market intelligence group, reported that multicultural consumers drove 78 percent of real total expenditures growth for ten years through 2012. Collage analysts calculated that multicultural consumers spent approximately eight in ten incremental real dollars during this period. Looking forward, Collage indicated that the multicultural population has the potential to drive up to 85 percent of total expenditure growth between 2016 and 2026, and during the next ten-year period, multicultural consumers will drive significant sales growth across all categories.

Collage further indicated that if the economy experiences anywhere between $730 billion and $2.4 trillion sales growth, multicultural consumers would be responsible for at least half of overall sales growth and show strong annual growth rates. This would certainly benefit the country's economy and American businesses specifically.

Revenue and Profit Potential

As with any consumer, demographic, cultural characteristics, and buying behavior can drive revenue potential. Capturing and maximizing this potential depends on how well companies mine relevant data and the efforts made to become familiar with multicultural consumers' consumption dynamics through both data and in-market observation. These steps are key to uncover, forecast, and validate sales growth among multicultural consumers for a given category and brand.

A 2016 Packaged Facts analysis highlighted several categories in which Hispanics drove a significant proportion of spending. It indicated that between 2012 and 2015, Hispanic households drove 40 percent of share growth for computers and telephones and 25 percent of share growth for new cars and trucks. Hispanic households also drove double-digit share growth in furniture (20 percent), major appliances (18 percent), audio-visual equipment and services (17 percent), and small appliances (16 percent).

Similar trends were seen in financial services. In the past ten years, the proportion of Hispanic individuals and households adopting an extensive array of financial services grew faster than among non-Hispanic consumers. For instance, between 2005 and 2015, Hispanics' credit-card use grew eleven times faster than among non-Hispanics (44 percent versus 4 percent). The 5.1 million additional Hispanics with credit cards accounted for half (49 percent) of the growth in the number of consumers using credit cards. Think of all the interest and fee income generated on purchases made with these new cards. At a time when companies are looking for organic growth and growth margins are slimmer than ever, this type of double-digit growth could be one of the solutions companies have been looking for.

This type of growth doesn't just happen, and it doesn't happen for all companies. It happens for companies that commit to expanding their strategies to multicultural markets and that align their organizations to implement innovatively and relevantly.

Notable Industry Wins

Let's examine some examples of the type of strategic thinking and management that has successfully led to top-line and market-share growth for some companies. These management examples are based on the Hispanic market, but the thinking and approaches are equally applicable to companies serving any other multicultural population.

Wireless Cell

Mark Stockdale led T-Mobile's entry and brand development among Hispanics for many years. Just after he had joined the company, he conducted a very thorough 360-degree internal and competitive assessment that included all major wireless providers; this was instrumental in level-setting the current industry situation at the time.

Stockdale said the wireless industry evolved into one of the largest beneficiaries of Hispanic spending power. Nearly two decades ago, two of the four current national wireless carriers began their journey to understand and engage Hispanic consumers. It quickly became clear that regardless of how the wireless industry evolved—whether a simple phone plan, a phone and text plan, or a phone, text, and data plan—higher usage patterns among Hispanics would be the norm. Fast forward to 2017, and according to Nielsen, Hispanics are 22 percent more likely to buy a smartphone in the next twelve months and 31 percent more likely to have spent $500 or more on their last smartphone purchase.

Nielsen Mobile Insights reports that Hispanics represented 63 percent of total net adds and 100 percent of total post pay net adds in Q2 2017 (the most recent report as of this writing). This represented a 4 percent increase in total net adds compared to 0 percent among non-Hispanics and a 5 percent increase in post pay net adds compared to a 1 percent decline among non-Hispanics.

The industry's key performance indicators (KPIs) consistently demonstrated the revenue potential. Hispanics typically over index non-Hispanics between 6 and 8 percent on average revenue per unit (ARPU). Measures like churn, which measures contract cancellations, are comparable to non-Hispanics, though this wasn't always the case. Right-fitting phones and contracts to Hispanics' needs have improved this metric considerably, irrespective of product-focus strategies—premium post-pay plans or pre-pay plans.

Stockdale stressed that most companies in the industry once experienced the same uphill battle of securing budgets to fund Hispanic market efforts but emphasized that methodical and rigorous analysis always validated and overcame internal reservations. Wireless companies soon learned that not all Hispanic households have low incomes and are, therefore, low value. Companies also learned that having no credit is not the same as having poor credit. Friendlier phone pricing and no-contract plans did much to address many of these hurdles.

KPI dashboards also helped companies stay focused on the business and reset cross-functional misinformed points of view when they surfaced. Stockdale likes to quote W. Edwards Deming, who said, "Without data, you're just another person with a point of view." For example, when demographic geotargeting analyses and same-store sales reports confirm that most locations in high Hispanic-density areas generate more revenue than non-Hispanic locations, it validates continued investment, including in new store openings.

Not surprisingly, many of the improvements made by companies to address dealer networks, store footprint, sales experience, plan enhancements, and accessibility also accelerated stronger Hispanic acquisition and retention. Stockdale added that higher adoption and usage rates are largely due to a few factors: Hispanics' younger profiles, making them more techno hungry; their large family networks in-country and abroad with which they stay connected; and their larger families in the United States, which require more lines.

Stockdale strongly advocates for analyzing the business to understand Hispanics' impact on revenue and share growth. He says the only way to truly understand how Hispanics' characteristics and cultural inclinations can lead to accelerated growth is to do the homework. With consistent study of business results and consumer response, the cellular industry benefits from Hispanics' strong spending trends and achieves robust sales results.

Grocery Retail

The large and growing Hispanic market has created tremendous affinity for Hispanic foods among non-Hispanic consumers, and food manufacturers have been happy to satisfy them. According to Package Facts, the Hispanic foods category is expected to grow from about $17.5 billion in 2015 to over $21 billion in 2020, a compound annual growth rate (CAGR) of 3.8 percent—higher than the CAGR of 2.9 percent through 2022 for the U.S. food industry overall. At the same time, spending for food at groceries and other food stores by Hispanic consumers grew more than 80 percent over the past decade, more than double the growth rate of non-Hispanics.

This profitable business growth trend has not gone unnoticed by Angel Colón, senior director of diversity, multicultural development, and supplier diversity at Kroger Co. Colón has been leading Kroger's multicultural success for over nine years. He characterizes the Hispanic shopper as "extremely profitable because they outspend the average consumer on spend per household—they are our dream customer." It's been a long journey, according to Colón, and he is no stranger to internal apprehensions about investing budgets to target Hispanic shoppers. He credits consistent category analysis and a constant eye on KPIs like dollar sales, profit margins, spend per household, market share, and Kroger's shopper study for the retailer's strong internal support. "When Hispanic and Asian efforts outpace the enterprise and result in incremental growth, the divisions take notice," said Colón. The growing affinity for ethnic foods among mainstream shoppers has also increased the organization's orientation toward ethnic foods to the extent that Kroger has integrated ethnic food brands into its respective categories because it makes sense with the way all its customers shop.

Package Facts projects spending by Hispanic food shoppers will reach $86 billion in 2018, representing a cumulative growth of more than 28 percent and a CAGR of more than 5 percent—almost twice the CAGR of 2.9 percent projected for the overall food industry. According to Package Facts, Hispanics place less emphasis on price point compared to consumers overall. This suggests that consumer packaged goods (CPG) brands and retailers that focus on meeting Hispanics' shopping needs are likely to accelerate top-line growth.

Colón said, "The company's focus on these consumers has never been greater. Marketing and merchandising pilots targeting multicultural shoppers are constantly tested and course-corrected based on insights, sales data, and consumer input." He adds, "For the last five years, most divisions want to implement on pilots quickly. I would even say that most departments now expect Hispanic market pilots to outperform the enterprise, and many departments are on cruise control. We're still providing proof of concept results, but there is no question at Kroger about their successful results."

Many CPG companies are seeing comparable results in their businesses. Santiago Solutions Group conducted a valuable analysis for the Association of Hispanic Advertising Agencies (AHAA) that points to a significant revenue growth rate among CPG companies and grocery retailers that strategically and consistently target Hispanic shoppers compared to companies that do not. AHAA's past president, Roberto Orci, said, "The difference between committed and uncommitted CPGs and retailers is that committed companies realize that Hispanic shoppers help deliver on two crucial business goals—winning market share from competitors and delivering growth and stability to shareholders. It's as simple as that."

Santiago Solutions analyzed the top U.S. advertisers between 2006 and 2010 and found, with a 95 percent confidence level, that among CPG brands, the share of overall dedicated marketing resources correlates with one-third of companies' overall revenue growth—a proportion that is twice the market's population size. Strategic companies and retailers including Coca-Cola, General Mills, Ralcorp, Groupe Danone, Nestlé, Walmart, and Walgreens demonstrated the highest overall organic revenue growth from their consistent and proportionate Hispanic market investments. The survey found Hispanics' household food-at-home expenditures were estimated to grow at a 5.7 percent average annual rate over the next ten years compared to just 2.5 for non-Hispanic households. This is consistent with CAGR projections for Hispanic food spending through 2018, as calculated by Packaged Facts.

The data is indisputable. Hispanics are a panacea for CPG and food-retail companies looking for accelerated top-line growth. CPG companies and food retailers that insist on remaining on the sidelines or are tentative about expanding their growth strategies to multicultural consumers need to seriously weigh the impact and cost of inaction on their revenue, market share, and value building.

Auto Aftermarket

Like most industries, the auto aftermarket industry is struggling to generate stronger organic growth, but a closer examination of the growing U.S. Hispanic consumer base and its DIY behavior reveals a significant top-line growth opportunity. Lisa Kranc, recent past senior vice president of marketing, and the AutoZone executive team saw value in expanding its strategy to the Hispanic market as AutoZone grew its store presence in areas where the car market was in its sweet spot—cars seven years or older—and realized these locations also had an overrepresentation of Hispanic populations.

Kranc and company stakeholders organized to target this consumer and kept a close watch on important KPIs, with sales being the most important. For example, the company segments its stores in a variety of ways to better understand sales dynamics, including looking at Hispanic versus non-Hispanic stores, and they've seen that Hispanic customers' sales contribution is extraordinary.

Internal analyses of AutoZone store sales relative to Hispanic market concentration are often performed, and there is a strong correlation between higher Hispanic population concentration and significantly higher per store sales compared to stores overall; stores where there is a high concentration of Hispanics generate sales in order of magnitude higher (20 to 50 percent higher) compared to stores with low to no Hispanics in the trade area. The same sales trend existed among AutoZone's commercial customer locations.

The Hispanic market has become a strategic imperative that involves the entire organization. Kranc said, "We knew this had to be more than a marketing initiative—it had to become a total company effort at the forefront of our strategic planning." While there were a couple of cases of internal resistance at the beginning, once the loyalty data was available, the resistance subsided. Kranc put it this way: "I didn't have to say very much to overcome the resistance even among the one or two hardcore resisters. The data spoke loudly in terms of how important this segment was, and resisters came around. It was objective data, and it was irrefutable. Also, it wasn't just one data set. Every data set confirmed the importance of Hispanics' contribution to our sales growth. It was consistent no matter how anybody looked at the data. We even did multivariate analysis, and that also pointed to sales upsides for the whole business. At this point, it wasn't about selling anybody on it. It was about actively collaborating to continue building on our sales success. The analytics and understanding the numbers kept the company aligned on this imperative."

The analysis became increasingly refined and focused once the company was able to draw on larger samples of Hispanic loyalty data and was able to see the specific items Hispanics purchased. These insights allowed the company to tailor its products and product sets in more targeted ways based on Hispanic customers' preferences. On the marketing side, Lisa and her team continued to test their marketing messages and media mix to ensure the spending and the mix were continuously optimized.

Hispanics' heavier spending on auto aftermarket items is due to a greater affinity to DIY behavior. DIY behavior is driven in part by lower incomes, more free time, and a sense of pride in being self-sufficient. The market's demographics and car-buying behavior also play a big part. The census indicates that every thirty seconds, two non-Hispanics hit retirement age, while one Hispanic turns eighteen. This step into adulthood often includes buying a car.

As it happens, Hispanics are driving car sales growth in the United States. In 2016, they spent $60 billion on new car purchases compared to $53 billion among non-Hispanics. Hispanic auto purchases are expected to double from 2010 to 2020, growing at a pace of 116 percent.

Hispanics bought just over two million new vehicles in 2016 and almost six million used cars—13.25 percent of all new vehicles and 14.25 percent of all used cars and trucks, respectively. Additionally, the Consumer Expenditure Survey published by the Bureau of Labor Statistics attributes a greater share of yearly used-car, gasoline, and motor-oil spending to Hispanics compared to total households, all of which bode well for auto-aftermarket and oil-company revenue and market-share growth.

Keeping an eye on demographics and complementary industry purchase trends can help retailers validate profit-growth opportunities in many industries, including the auto aftermarket. But companies must be willing to roll up their sleeves and triangulate data from various sources to uncover and validate the Hispanic market's extraordinary revenue potential.

Health Insurance

Until very recently, Russell Bennett was the VP of opportunity strategy and development for a business unit of UnitedHealthcare, and for many years (including prior to the acquisition of PacifiCare by UnitedHealthcare), he was VP of Latino initiatives. There is a fantastic case study of Bennett's Hispanic market achievements at PacifiCare in my first book, *Marketing to Hispanics—A Strategic Approach to Assessing and Planning Your Initiative*. Bennett indicated that for the last fifteen years, several health-insurance carriers have regularly analyzed the cost and health service utilization by Hispanic populations in health care and health insurance and consistently found that Hispanic members are less costly and therefore more profitable than non-Hispanics. These findings have helped those carriers forecast sales and profit potential across market characteristics such as age, geography, and product type.

Most health-insurance carriers sell policies to employer groups and charge a monthly premium (calculated to cover health-care costs and risks, sales, general and administrative expenses, and profits) to provide covered health benefits to the employees and their dependents. When health-insurance carriers can effectively manage health-care costs, which represent the largest portion of operating expenses, profits can be maximized. Of course, controlling selling, general, and administrative expenses (SG&A) is also critical to profitability.

Because the cost of acquiring and enrolling new members is significantly higher than retaining them, it's important that strategies are put in place to enhance members' experiences and satisfaction to maximize retention and minimize additional marketing costs. Bennett says, "Strategies should also emphasize member education about their health and health insurance because it leads to appropriate and cost-effective utilization, which stabilizes cost."

This type of profitability analysis looking at Hispanic and non-Hispanic members can help carriers (1) identify the most and least profitable employer groups, (2) identify the most and least profitable products and services, (3) identify which information sources about members are most reliable, (4) optimize response methods as customers' needs evolve, (5) maximize profits in the medium and long term by changing the product and marketing mix, and (6) isolate and leverage increasing profit margins.

Hispanic member profitability can be analyzed in several ways, including the following:

- Net Profit Margin — looks at how much of the company's sales revenue is kept as profit, the percentage of premium dollars received spent on medical costs, the percentage that goes to other operating expenses, and the percentage that flows to the bottom line
- Gross Profit Margin — calculated on a per-member-per-month basis (PMPM) by studying employer groups to identify which groups had higher gross-profit PMPM and ranking them according to the percentage of Hispanic members and dependents employed by the group
- Comparative Expense Analysis — review of medical expense ratios for Hispanic members versus non-Hispanic members
- Profit by Segment — profitability analysis of Hispanic members versus non-Hispanic members

Over more than fifteen years, Hispanic members have consistently exhibited between 18 and 20 percent lower medical cost ratios, contributed significantly to higher profitability for certain insurance carriers, measured as higher profitability on the employer groups and individuals, and contributed to the profitability of the geographic regions where Hispanic members and their employer groups are located.

Normalized for age bands and sex, these analyses have been done across various large-population, highly Hispanic states and across the national data, so the analyses yield reliable insights. Well-informed insurance carriers do these analyses across their full commercial portfolio, including small, medium, and large employer groups. Depending on the customer size segment, this lower medical cost ratio of Hispanic members helped leverage the profitability of that business segment.

For example, even where premiums are adjusted for health status, there is no adjustment for a lower propensity to use health services, so Hispanic members produced much higher profitability than average. When the higher margin was reflected across employer groups and geographic regions, it clearly demonstrated that all other factors being equal, higher proportions of Hispanic members in an employer group led to higher gross profit PMPM. Bennett explains that several factors lead to lower medical cost ratios, but the most significant is a propensity among Hispanics to have a lower average utilization rate of medical services as well as a higher average utilization of generic drugs rather than more expensive branded drugs.

As Hispanics join the labor force in considerable numbers across all industries, they are an increasingly important profit driver for employer groups and health-insurance carriers. This makes it critical for carriers to understand the needs and preferences of Hispanic members and ensure their organizations are optimized to provide positive and instructive member experiences that keep costs and health-service utilization at appropriate levels. Russell believes that constant analysis that considers and looks at profit potential across all members, whether general market or multicultural, is a key to driving profitable growth.

He adds, "It's important not to get hung up on nomenclature. The bottom line is that multicultural consumers are simply American consumers of other cultures. They are integral parts of consumer targets for any business, but they will not necessarily be reached or convinced to buy our products and services through generic approaches to branding and customer experiences. These consumers are, quite simply, American consumers with different mind-sets, tastes, and purchasing triggers, which must be understood and acted upon. Several industries have found and continue to find these diverse consumers are critical differentiators with the power to advance profitability and shareholder value."

Category Expenditure Drivers

The notable examples in the previous section demonstrate how four business categories have successfully leveraged the Hispanic segment of multicultural populations to achieve organic growth in a sustainable manner. To complement these examples, here is some proven data from the 2015–16 Consumer Expenditure Survey, showing (1) categories where Hispanic and Asian households spent more in absolute terms compared to total households and (2) categories where Hispanic and Asian households spent less in absolute terms than total households but spent a greater proportion of their respective total annual expenditures compared to total households.

Companies would benefit from familiarizing themselves with multicultural consumers' spending tendencies and sales potential for their categories and to determine how it may make sense to expand their strategies to these high-value populations.

Hispanic Households

According to the 2015–2016 Consumer Expenditure Survey, Hispanic households spent 7 to 38 percent more in absolute dollars compared to total U.S. households on several types of products and services, as indicated on Figure 2.1. Among others, Hispanic households spent more than total households on men's and boys' apparel, footwear, children's apparel, and cell service.

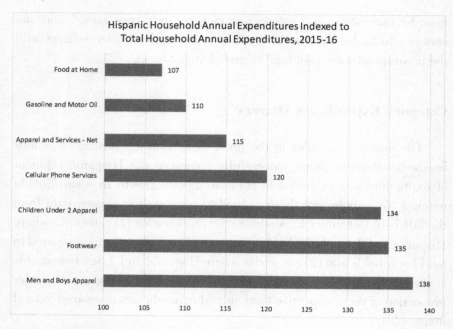

Source: 2015–2016 Consumer Expenditure Survey, Bureau of Labor Statistics

Figure 2.1. Hispanic household annual expenditures indexed
to total household annual expenditures (2015–16).

In similar categories, Hispanic households spent a greater proportion
of their total household expenditures compared to the proportion spent by
total households. Figure 2.2 shows the categories where Hispanic household
expenditures as a proportion of their total household expenditures were
6 to 72 percent greater. These included apparel, cellular services, and
much more on home furnishings, groceries, gasoline and motor oil, auto
insurance, and restaurants compared to the proportion on these types of
expenditures among total households.

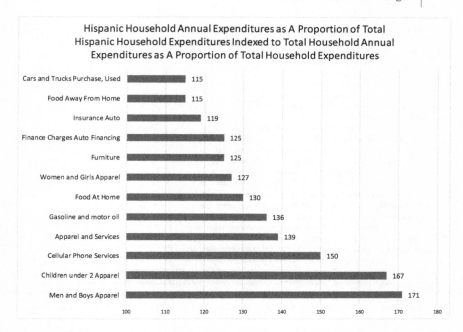

Source: 2015–2016 Consumer Expenditure Survey, Bureau of Labor Statistics

Figure 2.2. Hispanic household annual expenditures as a proportion of total Hispanic household expenditures indexed to total household annual expenditures as a proportion of total household expenditures.

Asian Households

The 2015–2016 Consumer Expenditure Survey also indicates that Asian households spent 7 to 99 percent more in absolute dollars compared to total households on many products and services, as indicated in Figure 2.3. Most notably, Asian household expenditures on education and public transportation were almost twice as much compared to total households.

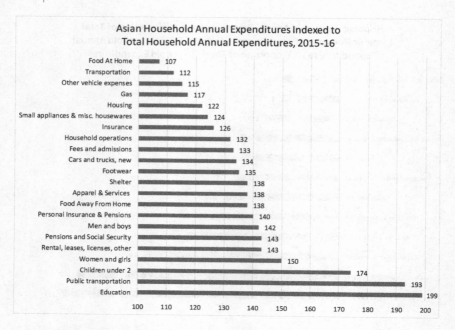

Source: 2015–2016 Consumer Expenditure Survey, Bureau of Labor Statistics

Figure 2.3. Asian household annual expenditures indexed to total household annual expenditures (2015–16).

In similar categories, Asian households spent a greater proportion of their total household expenditures compared to the proportion spent by total households. Figure 2.4 shows the categories where Asian household expenditures as a proportion of their total household expenditures are 7 percent to 99 percent greater. These include education, public transportation, new cars, restaurants, and apparel compared to the proportion on these types of expenditures among total households.

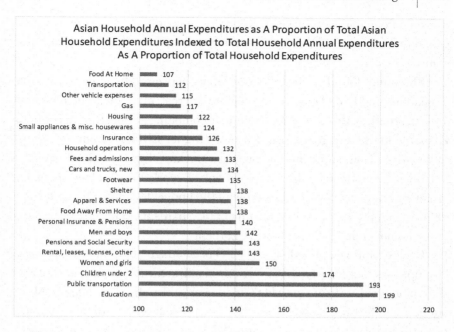

Asian Household Annual Expenditures as A Proportion of Total Asian
Household Expenditures Indexed to Total Household Annual Expenditures
As A Proportion of Total Household Expenditures

Category	Index
Food At Home	107
Transportation	112
Other vehicle expenses	115
Gas	117
Housing	122
Small appliances & misc. housewares	124
Insurance	126
Household operations	132
Fees and admissions	133
Cars and trucks, new	134
Footwear	135
Shelter	138
Apparel & Services	138
Food Away From Home	138
Personal Insurance & Pensions	140
Men and boys	142
Pensions and Social Security	143
Rental, leases, licenses, other	143
Women and girls	150
Children under 2	174
Public transportation	193
Education	199

Source: 2015–2016 Consumer Expenditure Survey, Bureau of Labor Statistics

Figure 2.4. Asian household annual expenditures as a proportion
of total household expenditures indexed to total household annual
expenditures as a proportion of total household expenditures.

Some companies are keenly aware of these consumption trends and are reaping the rewards of their consistent and focused efforts on expanding their strategies relevantly to these multicultural populations. Further proof of positive financial impact for committed companies was confirmed by Santiago Solutions Group in a study of 180 top national advertisers. The study was a correlation analysis of Hispanic marketing budget allocation and profitability. The study revealed that the top 25 percent of companies with the highest allocation to Hispanic marketing investment as a proportion of their marketing budgets generated 2.1 times higher bottom-line profitability (net income) than companies that invested less.

The top quartile of companies that invested a fair share to attract Hispanics to their brands generated higher cumulative shareholder value over the four-year period studied than the remaining 75 percent of companies. Each dollar invested in Hispanic marketing by these top 25 percent of companies returned four dollars. The top quartile of companies generated 1.5 times higher operating income margins than the remaining companies.

The study found a positive correlation between Hispanic marketing allocations and EBITDA (earnings before interest, taxes, depreciation, and amortization), with the top 25 percent of companies allocating budgets to Hispanic marketing generating 1.3 times higher EBITDA than the others in the study. Companies in the consumer-packaged goods (CPG) category led all other industries in their percent of marketing budget spent on targeting Hispanics, with 5.5 percent of the budget to Hispanic marketing; following on the list were entertainment (4.7 percent), retail (4.4 percent), and automotive manufacturers (4.1 percent).

Carlos Santiago, president and CEO of Santiago Solutions Group, says, "Companies that translate their Hispanic market investment into superior shareholder value do not merely throw money at the Hispanic market. More often, these leading companies adopt new allocation paradigms matched to the specific growth opportunity and have solid executive leadership, passionate doers at all levels, a solid strategic direction, and flawless action with accurate quantitative metrics. In short, the bottom-line value is so clear to these companies, they do it right, and they reap the financial rewards."

It's important to note that attracting multicultural populations to a brand, retaining them, and making them champions for a brand requires more than an allocation of marketing dollars. It requires a focused and coordinated effort to expand a company's strategy and delivering the strategy relevantly. This requires seamless integration of a new consumer group to day-to-day business operations.

Most savvy leaders know that retention is less expensive than acquisition. As such, retention through a positive and frictionless customer experience is a critical component in the delivery of a company's strategy and requires more than just the marketing department—it requires the entire organization.

Moreover, creating a positive and frictionless customer experience for multicultural consumers requires understanding multicultural populations as three-dimensional people, not just as two-dimensional numbers on a spreadsheet or as a description on a presentation. Companies must get to know these customers as well as they know themselves. Think about any reciprocal relationship, whether personal or business. The people involved need to understand and meet the needs of the person or persons from whom they want appreciation and loyalty. This is fundamental to the authenticity and integrity most people expect to gain their trust and loyalty.

Shareholder Value

The intrinsically linked relationship among organic revenue growth, strong shareholder value creation, and a position of market advantage in the $3.5 trillion multicultural market is clear. According to PricewaterhouseCoopers' annual CEO survey, most CEOs (92 percent) in 2017 point to organic growth as the number-one way to build value for their organizations. To achieve this effectively, CEOs believe they must leverage modern technologies and innovation as well as expand their existing operations to new markets.

Targeting multicultural populations in the United States fits squarely within CEOs' growth plans. Moreover, revenue growth experienced by companies with a strong multicultural population focus is already contributing to organic growth and value building for their organizations.

Perhaps the question progressive and visionary leaders should be asking now is how to leverage technological advances, innovation, and expansion efforts into new markets to accelerate value building even further in this country, where the multicultural population is so large, is growing so rapidly, and is so economically viable. The answer to this question becomes especially important as CEOs struggle with declining consumer trust and changing consumer needs, the latter being influenced in large part by increased multiculturalism. One way to address these issues is to consider today's broader definition of the country's demographics and use modern technology to innovate relevantly—and to do so in a well-informed and authentic manner.

Value-building strategies like cost reduction, divestitures, and exiting markets are quick ways to improve the bottom line in the eyes of Wall Street. Cutback strategies are sometimes appropriate, but most leaders recognize they shouldn't become automatic fallback positions because building value is fundamentally about making a brand more valuable to consumers, so they are more attractive and consumers want to do business with it more than with the competition.

Furthermore, organizing and investing in a company's ability to effectively compete in a new marketplace, where the consumer is different and evolving, aligns with value building not only domestically but also internationally. Companies with an international presence or those thinking about expanding their strategies internationally would benefit from developing their skills with multicultural populations domestically as it would prepare them for success internationally.

There is much to gain with this approach. It's no secret that some American companies that expand their operations internationally often struggle with cultural, societal, and political issues because managers' skills are limited to domestic environments and colleagues and consumers who look like them. Couple this with the often-held America-centric views that may judge other cultures and nations by American standards, and companies are up against high learning curves, long ramp-up periods, and even longer wait times to break even and profit.

CEOs and boards have multiple reasons to step up their multicultural market awareness and expertise in the United States, so they can leverage this knowledge to grow profits domestically and globally. As mentioned earlier in the chapter, many companies started to think about refocusing their attention and investment domestically several years ago as they increasingly view the United States as an emerging market with compelling population and consumption growth not seen in global markets to the degree it exists in the United States.

And the best part of this is that the largest emerging market of all is within U.S. borders. After all, 38 percent of the country's population is multicultural. This is an extraordinarily large number. Developing the skills to think, plan, and implement companies' business strategies in ways that consider diverse cultural, societal, economic, and political views has become an imperative, and strengthening leaders' cultural intelligence about multicultural populations in the United States has become a critical success factor. It's quite possible this could also bode well for growing shareholder value.

Economic Success Outlook

The economic outlook for American businesses that look to multicultural populations in the United States to accelerate revenue growth appears extremely favorable. Demographic and economic indicators including youth, birth rates, increasing education, increasing labor-force participation, entrepreneurship penetration, increasing incomes, and high consumption across key categories reinforce projections for continued revenue and profit growth for American businesses.

I'm reminded of Michael Porter's Five Forces Framework, which we all learned in business school. The framework proposes that the threat of new entrants is one of the most powerful forces that shapes the competitive structure of an industry and threatens profitability. Companies that have already expanded their strategies to multicultural markets and position their markets as a business imperative embody the "threat of new competition" for those companies that have yet to do so.

These companies are leveraging one of the most important value-creation tools any company could compete for—a new market, one that can accelerate revenue and market-share growth in the short term and contribute to profitable growth in the middle and long term.

Competitors enter this market in greater and greater numbers all the time and represent a formidable competitive threat to companies that continue to sit idle or make ad hoc and sporadic efforts to capture this business.

The question to ask at this pivotal time in marketing history is whether you will be among the companies that wait to see sales history written by your competitors or whether your company will be among those that position their organizations leverage multicultural population trends to make sales history.

Chapter 3

Multicultural Realities

Companies that are benefiting from expanding their strategies to multicultural populations in the United States have achieved a dominant business advantage. These companies have always been just as challenged by multiple priorities and growth pressures as other companies. Their leadership is similarly tasked to accomplish much with limited time, people, and budgets; the difference is that for these leaders, the incremental revenue potential of multicultural markets is so crystal clear that successfully expanding and delivering their strategy to multicultural populations became an imperative.

Stalling or Stalled

While a select group of companies reap the benefits multicultural populations offer, an overwhelming number of companies are stalling or are completely stalled in this regard. For some, multicultural population is still off the radar, and many others are still unsure about the value multicultural populations represent. I often hear leaders making contradicting comments that suggest they recognize the value multicultural populations represent, but the rest of the organization does not or is unaware. Their apprehension and uncertainty is palpable when making comments such as the following:

- "We don't want to call too much attention to this initiative in case it doesn't work."
- "We want to make sure this work is not too disruptive or requires too many resources."
- "We need to keep it low-key because we don't want to upset folks internally."
- "We need to be light-handed in our implementation in our retail locations because we don't want to upset our core customers."

Taken out of context, one might think they're referring to some shady activity rather than efforts to potentially generate revenue growth for the company. This type of tentativeness is often the result of an effort driven by a single individual or a department. However, revenue growth initiatives for a company cannot be born in and confined to the purview of one person or one department. To gain the sustained support to expand the company's strategy to multicultural markets in a way that aligns with the company's direction and focus requires top-level–driven analysis and a due-diligence process that makes a strong business case for undertaking the effort.

Getting to this stage has proven challenging for many companies that struggle with ill-planned and implemented initiatives. It is a difficult step to take when leadership hasn't acknowledged and has little familiarity with multicultural markets.

As a result, a sizable number of U.S. companies have yet to organize to take advantage of the revenue potential among multicultural consumers. In 2015, the CMO Council surveyed their CMO, SVP, and marketing VP members about their activities to target multicultural populations. The study found that on average, half of survey companies had no organized initiative or investment to capture sales in multicultural markets. Only two-thirds of business-to-consumer (B2C) companies and 20 percent of business-to-business (B2B) companies reported some type of activity. The B2B finding is particularly counterintuitive given the 39 percent growth in minority-owned business between 2007 and 2012 (from 5.8 million to 8.0 million) compared to 3 percent growth among total U.S. firms during the same period.

CMO Council survey participants cited an array of reasons for not investing in expanding their strategies to multicultural markets. Half reported "too many competing priorities," while "budget and resource limitations" precluded another third from focusing on this market. Another fourth of respondents believed their company is "already effectively targeting multicultural consumers through existing strategies"—a common but often incorrect assumption. Over one-third cited several other reasons, including, "not everyone being on board," "the field not understanding the importance," or "management not being sold on the idea."

When only 10 percent of managers place blame on the company's leadership for not supporting the expansion of their strategies to multicultural markets and "competing priorities" and "budget limitations" are cited as primary reasons for inaction, it is the survey participant themselves who are unaware or unconvinced about the revenue impact to their businesses.

Oftentimes the C-suite may be convinced that the business potential exists and may be taking steps to mobilize and organize the company to target the market, but efforts fail to gain traction at the CMO, VP, and director levels, where strategy implementation and budgets are controlled.

It's not enough to announce the expansion of a company's strategy to multicultural markets is an imperative; senior leadership must organize and follow through to implement it successfully. There are several very important steps management must take to ensure traction:

1. Ensure implementers understand the nature of the effort. The goal is to expand the company's existing strategy to the multicultural population, not to develop a new strategy.
2. Support and fund the upfront business development analysis and due diligence and engage top leadership to use the analysis to develop and communicate the business case.
3. Support the development of cultural awareness, sensitivity, and competency among key people and departments so new consumer targets are understood as people and as consumers.
4. Define the process by which the new market will be integrated into everyday planning and implementation (this is not a stand-alone initiative).
5. Assign oversight responsibility to a top-level decision maker. This person would be assigned by the president or CEO and would have the power to make people and budget decisions.

6. Establish and communicate accountability metrics and KPIs.
7. Define good implementation performance and define the rewards.

When the above steps are absent, middle management will focus on what they know, and the expansion to multicultural markets will be optional or of secondary importance to responsibilities for which they are being held accountable and rewarded, and they will make implementation and budget choices that are consistent with these priorities.

When those responsible for implementation are not set up to succeed, choices will be driven by lack of understanding, fear of mistakes from unfamiliarity with a new market, and the need to protect professional agendas. Even when business leaders have a keen awareness of multicultural market insights and the business potential, there is still the chance they will default to focus on more familiar core consumers whom they've been tasked to attract, satisfy, and protect.

The absence of a clear plan and senior leadership oversight will discourage these managers from championing or "signing their name" to unproven initiatives that might fail or not produce results soon enough. Managers will always choose to focus on projects where they feel confident of the results and where their reputation, raise, and next promotion will not be jeopardized. Fear of the unknown and risk aversion are the two most common distractors among managers assigned to manage multicultural growth efforts, especially when established priorities for which they are being rewarded are tugging at them.

An argument could be made that managers whose training and focus are on protecting the core business may not be appropriately matched to efforts that focus on expanding a strategy to a new consumer market. One could argue that the goals are protecting core consumers or defending market share and expanding the core and growing market share and competing priorities. Expanding a company's strategy to a new market where the company sees the potential to increase revenue and market share is a very different job from protecting core customers and current market share. The first requires an intrapreneurial mind-set and business-building skills. It also requires senior leadership involvement and a team with clarity of the business case, goals, and specific rewards for meeting milestones and hitting the metrics. A strategy-expansion effort needs to be managed accordingly. And this is what makes it so important for implementers to have clarity of business goals, strategies, and implementation approaches from the beginning.

From time to time, I run into leaders who adamantly reject the idea of aligning strategy implementation to the needs of a group of consumers who may be different from the company's idea of their core consumer. It's quite difficult to influence these strongly held beliefs, but it's important to note that this thinking tends to come from a place of uncertainty and a lack of knowledge about consumers who are seen as different.

Interestingly, multicultural consumers' consumption dynamics are not so different from those of whom a company considers their core consumer. Oftentimes a lack of cultural awareness and competency is what leads managers to think that cultural-dynamics differences are diametrically opposed rather than simple cultural nuances. This is the reason cultural development and building cultural intelligence is critical to setting up expansion efforts for success. It prevents implementers from dwelling on unrealistic notions of a vastly different consumer that would cloud their ability to see the business potential of a new consumer market.

When I speak to executive groups, I know there are folks in the room who have personal ideologies, political views, and reservations about the changing population and harbor ideas about vast differences in these growing populations. But these ideas and apprehensions quickly dissipate with a bit of education. The best thing to do when managers experience fear and hesitancy about a market they may think is too different is to validate multicultural consumers' value to revenue growth. I find an exercise I call the **Revenue Predictor GPS™** very helpful in putting this question into perspective. It is a helpful guide to conducting the business-development analysis and due diligence for the business case.

Working through this exercise will provide an objective way to analyze the multicultural opportunity as it relates to the business. The exercise involves some number crunching and interim steps to complete, but it helps managers objectively assess multicultural consumers as simply another revenue opportunity. The exercise works because it applies the same analysis process and criteria applied to assess any revenue potential market.

When Bennett, who led the strategy expansion into Hispanic and multicultural markets at UnitedHealthcare, said in Chapter 2, "It's important not to get hung up on nomenclature. The bottom line is that multicultural consumers are simply 'American consumers of other cultures.' These consumers are, quite simply, American consumers with different mind-sets, tastes, and purchasing triggers that must be understood and acted upon," he was speaking to the heart of this exercise.

Think about it. Multicultural consumers *are* just consumers. If you forget about race, ethnicity, culture, and language for a moment and analyze them logically and in a business context, you'll find they have the power to grow your sales and market share and make yourself look good! Read through the exercise, work through each step, and then write down your responses so you can see the results and have them available to share with other members of your team and senior leaders. You'll be surprised at how much more familiar multicultural consumers will appear once you reduce their characteristics to their revenue potential essence.

At the very least, this exercise should help you define the market's worth to the business and what you can gain or lose by tapping or ignoring it. Once you and senior leadership have vetted the potential and have assigned the right team and the appropriate budget to the effort, you'll be well on your way to capturing incremental sales.

Revenue Predictor GPS™

1. Start with your company's goals, strategies, and implementation focus.
2. Describe the characteristics of your core consumer.
3. Determine if the size of this core consumer is growing or declining in your trade areas and the cause of the growth or decline.
4. Determine how this growth or decline of the core-consumer population will impact achieving the goals based on high, medium, and low sales projections.
5. Determine which segment(s) of the multicultural population is most like your core consumer—demographics and consumption patterns.

6. Make some high, medium, and low sales projections to determine the incremental revenue and likely market-share growth within company time frames.

Define the aggregate and incremental value of multicultural targets vis-à-vis nonmulticultural targets to determine the short- and long-term impact on the business.

Companies in Action

While some leaders deliberate on the value of targeting multicultural consumers, others are actively pursuing them, albeit to varying degrees. Of CMO Council survey companies reporting an organized multicultural initiative, half unsurprisingly see management as the catalyst. Of those, 70 percent credited brand managers, 66 percent credited CMOs, almost half credited CEOs, and 40 percent credited the executive committee and the board of directors. This clearly speaks to the power of senior leadership's involvement in propelling these efforts forward. Upper management also plays a critical role in the effort's sustainability because like any other market entry, success requires the investment of resources.

It's important for companies to position their strategy expansion as a pillar to achieving the company's business goals. The CMO Council survey reported that only one-third of survey companies characterize their multicultural initiatives as "strategic," while another third call them "experimental." Experimental and test-and-learn methods are common among companies and can prove valuable to companies new to multicultural targeting or those seeking input to evolve their strategies.

"Experimental and test-and-learn methods are especially productive when used to fine-tune initiatives before scaling them," explains Angel Colón, senior director of diversity, multicultural development, and supplier diversity at Kroger Co. He adds, "Kroger creates pilots for most of our marketing and merchandising concepts, including those targeting multicultural customers." Colón explains that pilots might be tested in one store, in several stores, in a region, and then nationally in a variety of relevant forms—and all the while, the concepts are fine-tuned according to sales results and consumer feedback. Used in this manner, experimental and test-and-learn approaches can be extremely valuable.

However, test-and-learn activity can also be unproductive when not employed properly or for the right reasons. For example, some companies engage in test-and-learn approaches with little preparation and unrealistic expectations and assumptions. Often test-and-learn activity is deployed as an experiment (or a series of experiments) with no parameters or benchmarks. When these "experiments" fail to produce expected results, companies abandon expansion efforts prematurely rather than using the learnings to adjust and try again. Often "failed" test-and-learn experiences lead companies to conclude that targeting multicultural markets was a mistake. Oftentimes companies' test-and-learn efforts are nothing more than "better than nothing" translations of advertising. Other times, a company will make a onetime media buy and expect to magically build awareness and purchase consideration from a two-to three-week flight with very low weight levels. These are exercises in futility and a waste of good money. I equate these efforts to throwing spaghetti against the wall to see if it sticks. It never does.

In other cases, companies do the work to get the message and the media right, but the company ignores the required internal operational alignment that ensures a positive customer experience in-store, online, or on the phone. The marketing may convince multicultural consumers to visit the store, make the phone call, or go online, but irrelevant customer experiences may fail to close the sale.

Advertising is a vital component for engaging consumers, multicultural and otherwise, but advertising alone does not contribute to revenue growth and retention. A company must be able to walk their talk, as the saying goes. When a company focuses on communications to drive sales and ignores the rest of the value chain, it is very difficult to demonstrate an understanding and appreciation of the new consumer target because the company will be unable to deliver its strategy relevantly—the customer promise in the advertising will not match the experience, therefore jeopardizing customer expectations and retention. Advertising efforts will increase brand awareness and improve imagery, but the full impact of a campaign is significantly undermined when the customer experience is under optimized and delivers a less-than-consistent-and-accessible customer experience.

Some companies also call sporadic efforts "test and learn" because they're often implemented with small and fluctuating budgets when and if those budgets can be found. These companies pop in and out of the market as budgets permit. For obvious reasons, these types of activities are seldom productive. Long gaps between efforts don't allow them to build on each other. There is little continuity, and they're unproductive because the lack of internal coordination precludes having back-end operations at the ready to support sporadic multicultural ad efforts. Companies typically think long and hard about their business models and how they will help the organization succeed. It's equally important to think long and hard about whether the business model is optimized to maximize sales opportunities among new and existing multicultural customers. Think about it. If it has been proven that the multicultural population or segments thereof can significantly contribute to revenue growth, it behooves the company to organize relevantly to win and keep the business.

The CMO Council survey also depicts marketers' under allocation of budgets. Three-fourths of surveyed companies allocate less than 15 percent of total budgets to multicultural efforts; of these, one-fourth allocated between 5 and 10 percent, and another fourth allocated less than 5 percent of total budgets. Half of survey companies said they allocate budgets based on "what is required to reach company goals, based on ROI and based on the size of multicultural targets as a proportion of the target overall." One-fourth of managers based their budget allocation on "the company's expected future growth," while 6 percent said they "benchmark against the competition." Chapter 2 describes Hispanic and Asian Households outspending non-Hispanic white households across many categories and shows where Hispanic and Asian household expenditures are a disproportionately larger piece of their annual expenditures compared to total households. Yet budgets are not being allocated to capitalize on Hispanic and Asian households' higher rates of spending.

One in four survey companies said attracting multicultural consumers is "mission critical." Yet just 5 percent of survey respondents who reported multicultural efforts as "mission critical" said they are "mandatory" and "unanimously embraced across the organization." It follows that there are higher levels of budget commitments among this 5 percent of respondents—one-fourth of the "mission critical" 5 percent allocated 16 percent or more, and 14 percent allocated more than 26 percent of their budgets to multicultural activity.

Surveyed companies also reported a variety of approaches to manage their multicultural efforts. Just over half said they employ a "total market" approach where all cultures are integrated and addressed with pooled resources. Multicultural initiatives that combine Hispanic, Asian, and African American consumers with separate resources and a separate staff from general-market efforts were used by 17 percent of the companies. One in ten companies had a separate initiative for Hispanic, Asian, and African American consumers with separate resources and staff for each, and 7 percent said they had a Hispanic marketing initiative with separate resources and staff.

Total-market approaches are certainly catching on. If implemented in earnest and by multicultural-market–competent managers, they can drive budget efficiencies and aligned results. The adoption of a total-market approach by over half of survey companies explains how half of the companies claimed their budget allocations are enough to attract and retain multicultural consumers. Companies should be cautious not to readily adopt the total-market approach before understanding the implication and evaluating whether it's in the company's best interest or whether it is being adopted because it is more budget efficient and easier to implement. In the end, it's about understanding the business case, organizing internally to integrate multicultural efforts into the business, and allocating the necessary resources to target the new market successfully.

Corporate Leader Archetypes

Leaders of American companies have distinct positions on what they are willing to do and invest to capture multicultural sales. One might even say there are corporate leader archetypes. Carl Jung, Swiss psychologist, argued that the root of an archetype is in the "collective unconscious" of mankind. "Collective unconscious" refers to experiences shared by a race or a culture. This includes love, religion, death, birth, life, struggle, survival, and so on. These experiences exist in the subconscious of every individual.

Similarly, there are underlying and unconscious experiences that lead certain leaders to acknowledge and appreciate the value of consumers of cultures that are different from their own and to value their respective revenue contributions to their brands. These unconscious experiences often include upbringing, past experiences, corporate culture, espoused beliefs of the organization, and personal ideologies.

As an advisor to senior executives in large American corporations, I've come across three archetypes in terms of their perception and outlook of multicultural populations, the value they assign to them, and the resulting effort and investment they will allocate to attract multicultural sales. These archetypes include the "deniers," the "dabblers," and the "committed." These archetypes are based on professional experience with dozens of Fortune 1000 companies and hundreds of conversations with clients, prospects, and colleagues over the last thirty years in practice.

The intent of sharing these archetype characteristics is to shed light on the types of archetype thinking and behavior that exists in corporate America. These archetype descriptions are intended to cause some reflection on where leaders might see themselves today, whether it is warranted, and how they may want to evolve their thinking and actions.

The Deniers

Deniers see the demographic change happening around them, but they don't think it's important to acknowledge it. They deny the changes they see will have any impact on them or their companies. They don't believe in adapting their business propositions to other cultures because according to them, other cultures should be adapting to them if they desire to do business with them. Deniers believe multicultural consumers are free to access, buy, and use their products and services the same way as anyone else, and if language is a barrier, they should learn to speak English. Among deniers, the customer-centric values that work to continuously enhance the customer experience don't apply to multicultural consumers if it means they need to adjust or change.

Culturally competent leaders will say, "We will meet our customers where they are, and we will find out what it takes to get them to desire and buy our product." Deniers don't see the value of applying this same mind-set to attract multicultural consumers. Deniers plan to hold out until all multicultural consumers speak English and look and behave like their core customers.

Deniers believe their number-one priority is keeping their core customers engaged and happy, even as that core base is shrinking across many categories. They have concerns about alienating their core customers by doing anything that might call too much attention and upset them. Some deniers believe that any sign of multicultural efforts or even the presence of multicultural customers in their stores upsets their core, so they do nothing.

For example, even though the average age of the non-Hispanic white female population is much older and they are having fewer children or are no longer in childbearing years, makers of female hygiene and baby products insist that organic growth will continue to come from focusing resources on their core customer—despite multicultural womens' younger profiles and significantly higher birth rates. One might argue that this approach is counterintuitive, but this is how deniers think.

Deniers refuse to face the long-term implications of how their targets will evolve. Peter Francese, founder of *American Demographics* magazine, made an astute observation during one of our conversations about the denier archetype. He said, "Denier archetypes focus on protecting the status quo. They play defense, but winning also requires playing offense— anticipating the next play or big market change and then adapting to it. Deniers are playing a dangerous game. Look at what happened to Eastman Kodak. They protected their print business when the industry was going digital until they practically died."

Defending the status quo at all costs puts a company at risk of becoming obsolete and irrelevant. Eastman Kodak is just one example. The giant faltered in the face of advancing technology. It defended the status quo until it fell so far behind consumer trends that it had to file for bankruptcy and is still struggling to recover. Now Kodak describes itself as a technology company. Borders bookstore was late to get serious about e-books. Blockbuster video-store chain didn't move quickly into streaming technology and was edged aside by Netflix. The list of companies that didn't adapt to changing consumer needs and wants grows longer all the time.

Many deniers believe in refrains such as "If it ain't broke, don't fix it" and "Leave well enough alone" as winning formulas in business. There's a belief that defending the status quo especially when business is good is the way to go. It isn't.

Deniers tend to be complacent because they claim to "be getting them [multicultural customers] anyway." Rather than capitalize on their strengths to accelerate growth in multicultural markets even further, they believe they have the option of doing nothing because they believe multicultural consumers already do or will eventually shop for them or their products.

Deniers ignore how quickly markets can shift when new competitors see the value of targeting and instilling loyalty among multicultural consumers. They ignore the need to constantly grow by finding future revenue streams and instead remain fixated on driving current profit margins—great strategy for the short term but not so good for the long term. By refusing to look at the shifting marketplace, they introduce significant risk from changes in the market, customer demand, and competitive activity.

Jim Kilts, one of the most renowned turnaround CEOs in corporate America, says, "I tell my employees, 'You must wake up every day, go into the office, and recognize there are people across the street, across the country, and across the globe who are trying to figure out how to get your business.'"

Organic growth is challenging, especially in mature industries where revenue eventually slows or even stalls. Innovation helps, but new consumer markets—multicultural markets—where a company's products are in demand are one of the strongest sources of growth for companies. Denying the country's demographic reality is shortsighted and counterproductive to a company's economics.

While some deniers are willing to expand abroad because such actions are important to improving investor-community perception, they overlook that investment requirements abroad can be significant and the time frames to breaking even, not to mention ROI, are long. Such ventures are not always favorable relative to building real company value in the short term.

The Dabblers

Dabblers are the most common type of archetype in corporate America. Dabblers are intrigued by but not completely convinced of the revenue contribution multicultural consumers represent to their organizations. Dabblers are the most likely to engage in experimenting and test-and-learn efforts. Dabblers are tentative, skeptical, and apprehensive about the value of targeting multicultural consumers versus their core market.

Dabblers that target multicultural consumers often look for shortcuts to results and want these efforts to be turnkey. They delegate responsibility for multicultural activity to junior brand associates and to multicultural ad agencies. From time to time, they parachute into progress meetings and briefings expecting big results despite minimal investments of time and budgets.

Dabblers continuously look for case studies and best practices as templates they can adopt to find proof of concept externally and avoid the effort of doing the market assessment and due-diligence work internally. More recently, dabblers are asking for the multicultural market "playbook" not as a guide but as a one-size-fits-all solution. Dabblers often engage in a host of shortsighted approaches that rarely work or are sustainable. Here are a few of them:

- **The Common Denominator** — Dabblers focus on insights that support their view that multicultural consumers are the same as existing core customers. This allows them to justify they already reach and cater to multicultural consumers' needs with current efforts. As a result, these efforts have minimum or no impact at all.
- **Self-Fulfilling Prophecy** — Dabblers invest minimally to target multicultural consumers because they believe multicultural results won't be as strong or as valuable as among their "core" customers. Results end up being weaker as a result.
- **Test and Learn** — Dabblers launch under supported and underfunded test initiatives with secret expectations for huge results, but they do it under the guise of "testing and learning" to minimize their exposure and accountability. They learn very little, and the results are mixed, but they save face.

Quick and Dirty — Dabblers develop quick and dirty multicultural ad campaigns. They rely on media partners for the market intelligence and are attracted by turnkey execution that can get them on the air "tomorrow" with minimal involvement and minimal time and budget investment. This approach saves money, time, and aggravation. The advertising lacks relevant insights and lacks connection to the overall marketing direction, the media buy is small, and the results are so disappointing that months or years go by before the company tries again—ironically in the same manner.

The Drive-By — The dabbler's brand has no awareness among multicultural consumers, but they decide to do a couple of promotions during key "relevant" holidays—a Cinco de Mayo or Kwanzaa or Chinese New Year event. No media or in-store support is given, and the promotion fails. They conclude that promotions don't work among multicultural consumers.

Dabblers constantly test a myriad of internal-structure and agency-relationship arrangements to minimize their involvement. It is the archetype known for engaging in the shortsighted efforts described earlier in the chapter. Dabblers don't commit; they're always giving up, and they're always starting over. As a result, their results in multicultural markets never seem to work as expected.

The Committed

Committed archetypes typically work for multinational organizations and have a keen sense of international markets and their consumer potential. Multinational companies are most likely to have a global view of the consumer market and can readily apply international experiences to multicultural populations in the United States. These companies include, among others, P&G, McDonald's, Walmart, Johnson & Johnson, Coca-Cola, Nestlé, Mars, and Unilever.

Committed leaders are often found in U.S. telecom and media companies, all of which experienced explosive demand for their services as multicultural populations in the United States grew. Multicultural population growth translated into demand to connect with the relatives they left behind. High telephone expenditures, large proportions of cable and satellite TV subscriptions to stay informed with news and sports and other entertainment from countries of origin, and insatiable mobile connectivity that far outpaces the nonmulticultural market because of the market's youthfulness were not lost on large providers like AT&T, Dish, Comcast, Verizon Wireless, and T-Mobile. These companies were quick to identify the multicultural opportunities and responded with targeted efforts. AT&T was perhaps the earliest adopter as demand for long-distance telephone service exploded in the 1980s and 1990s. Some automotive, financial-services, entertainment, fast-food, and insurance industries have also demonstrated themselves to have committed and long-term targeting efforts in place and, as a result, have seen tremendous top-line and market-share growth from multicultural consumers. Committed companies are continuously mobilizing their organizations to achieve company-wide commitment to the evolving multicultural marketplace.

Leading efforts to expand a company's strategy to a new consumer market, whether domestically or internationally, is a significant business undertaking that needs to be approached in a methodical and well-planned manner. Companies interested in capitalizing on the revenue potential this market represents must position their expansion efforts for success in the same manner as any other expansion effort.

The requirements include conducting the proper due diligence to define the opportunity and target consumer, setting appropriate goals and KPIs, having active CEO involvement, having senior leaders assigned to steward the effort, having cross-functional responsibility to deliver the strategy relevantly, and assigning budgets that are commensurate to the effort.

Chapter 4

Multicultural Marketing Evolution

Multicultural marketing has been evolving for the last thirty years but not in the way we might think. Agencies, market-research companies, syndicated data services, consultants, and the media have become impressively competent and sophisticated about the country's vastly different consumer markets, and their enthusiasm to help corporate clients capture the incremental revenue opportunity this market represents is as fervent as ever. However, many corporate clients remain stuck at the elementary level in terms their knowledge and appreciation of multicultural consumers, their vision on expanding their strategies to multicultural markets, and the commensurate investment to implement them relevantly and sustainably.

Over the last thirty years, as companies have attempted to attract multicultural consumers to their brands, they have not necessarily implemented the necessary business-development and due-diligence analysis to define the business case. More often, companies that start targeting multicultural consumers are reacting to requests from leadership. These requests jump-start managers into harried action based on what made sense given at the time. This lack of proper analysis and resulting small budgets has often lead to hasty implementation. This type of implementation has resulted in a broad spectrum of execution tactics to save money and time, including the following:

1. Translations of existing creative work—oftentimes translated by the first Spanish-speaking employee they come across
2. Media-led marketing
3. Sponsorships of turnkey community events or on-air radio promotions
4. Hiring an agency to execute mandated activity based on the company's ideas of what might work

Bottom line: the decision to target multicultural markets has typically been hasty and not preceded by a thorough due-diligence and planning process and a well-thought-out strategy-expansion plan that addresses organizational, infrastructure, and operational implementation implications. Any client company deciding for the first time to target multicultural consumers or that recognizes the need to put their multicultural efforts on more solid footing should begin by answering the following questions and using the answers to calibrate existing efforts.

Assessment and Planning

1. What are the company's current business priorities and strategies?
2. Who are the company's current consumers, and what characteristics make them ideal targets?
3. What proportion of Hispanic, Asian, African American, and Arabic consumers share similar characteristics as the company's current targets?
4. How much incremental consumption and revenue contribution can be attributed to these consumers?

Decision

5. Does it make sense to expand the company's strategies to these new markets? If so, which segments? Which products or services? Which divisions or business units?

Approach

6. What type of implementation alignment will need to take place to expand the strategy to these new markets?
7. What processes are needed to help integrate the alignment work within the organization, including operations, e.g., touch points and the back end that supports them?
8. Who will lead this expansion? What businesses and functions will support the expansion?
9. What type of competency training will be necessary to build internal knowledge and appreciation of new consumer targets?
10. What resources and budgets will be allocated incrementally to implement the expansion?

Metrics

11. What accountability metrics and mechanism will be in place to ensure continuity and sustainability?
12. How will we know the expansion is a success?
13. What type of milestones are expected and when?

It's important for companies to think about these new consumer targets in the context of existing business strategies and existing strategy implementation. Note that I'm saying "existing strategies." This is important because many companies that start to market to multicultural consumers don't realize that attracting these new consumers to their brands does not require a new strategy or business model. What it does require is implementation of the company's strategies in a manner that considers what is known about the new target segment and implementing relevantly.

However, because marketers lacked and still often lack this expertise and because the due-diligence process is not typically done, many companies still think they must do something completely different. They simply didn't know any better, and many still don't. And because the agencies they hire are asked to recommend what makes sense based on their knowledge of the market and very little about the company's focus, they often make very target-relevant recommendations though not necessarily aligned to the company's priorities.

As a result, companies often invest in efforts that are likely not aligned with the company's direction and its implementation plans. This is one of the primary reasons many multicultural budgets are often small, are often reduced, or often disappear when the company is looking for places to cut expenses.

Another symptom that stems from lack of proper upfront analysis and planning is the arbitrary allocation of marketing budgets that often don't align with the proportionately larger contributions multicultural consumers are making to sales growth or that they have the potential to contribute, as shown in Chapter 2.

For instance, *Ad Age* reported a total of $207.6 billion in ad spending in 2016, with total general-market advertising spending at $198 billion and Hispanic ad spending at $9.6 billion or 4.6 percent of the overall. It can be estimated that this is the largest proportion of multicultural ad spending as Asian and African American ad-spending totals are not tracked or available. Hispanic digital spending was 2.8 percent of the total $71 billion digital spending. The population size notwithstanding, the disparity is confounding considering the significantly younger and significantly more digitally engaged multicultural population.

A third symptom resulting from lack of analysis and planning is thinking that a company's core target and its multicultural target are separate and serve to achieve different objectives. Ironically, this may end up as the result when companies execute efforts that are not aligned with the company's goals, strategies, and implementation.

Companies' only solid rationale for targeting multicultural consumers should be that they represent a sizable base of consumers with similar consumption characteristics as existing core targets and offer, at minimum, a proportionate revenue and market-share growth advantage. When this criterion is met, this consumer becomes part and parcel of a company's core target.

At this point, budget-allocation criteria to reach, engage, serve, and retain this new consumer relevantly becomes much simpler to define. However, it's important to consider that relevant implementation requires optimizing back-end operations that support customer touch points, not just marketing.

Moving away from the ad hoc approach companies have used for decades requires companies to stop putting the proverbial cart before the horse and adopt a business-planning mentality to define whether to target multicultural segments and how. To do so, companies must treat efforts targeted to multicultural consumers as strategy-expansion efforts; they must develop their managers' cultural intelligence and their appreciation for diverse populations, and they must ensure they can service and satisfy the new consumers they attract.

The Agency–Client Divide

Because client companies haven't often had the expertise and appreciation for consumers of diverse cultures and because they are always pressed for time and managing multiple priorities, multicultural market responsibilities are often delegated to multicultural managers or to junior brand associates. This is a very risky management approach for multicultural efforts that often don't start off with sound strategic foundations or directions and that are tentative and arbitrary depending on other priorities.

Expanding into new consumer markets requires leadership from a business-unit vice president, a business director, or a senior brand manager because these individuals have a handle on company direction and priorities. Otherwise, it's like the blind leading the blind, and the expansion will be handicapped from the beginning and seriously affect how new consumer segments are integrated into the business. Management dynamics and decision making need to encompass the following actions:

1. Setting direction and defining how integration work is organized and monitored across the business(es)
2. Modeling leadership and commitment to business and functional areas related to new consumer segments
3. Aligning agency partners to the business's goals and strategies and integrating them to the overall implementation plans
4. Allocating resources based on assessment and modeling work
5. Performance measures and rewards
6. Making and supporting timely course-correcting decisions

Internal teams and external agency partners require leadership on important new market entries so they aren't left to create direction and execution in a vacuum only to have required resources denied.

Additionally, when multicultural agency leadership is included in company planning meetings and briefings, they can provide the necessary expertise about the new targets. Moreover, multicultural agencies can provide invaluable insight to guide the work in progress before it is finalized, providing two important benefits:

1. It ensures implementation relevance across marketing, customer experience, and the product and service.
2. It avoids retrofitting alignment work, which costs time and money and may lead to the work being abandoned.

Multicultural agencies that take part in planning can better align with their clients' priorities. They learn about KPIs that the company plans to monitor and the growth drivers the company has identified and plans to support, including specific brands, line extensions, divisions, or geographies that represent significant opportunity for growth. Moreover, knowing the client's big picture enables multicultural agencies to refine multicultural targets to reflect high-value customer profiles relative to focus brands, and it allows for better alignment between a brand's compelling value proposition and advertising concepts.

The absence of leadership involvement and agency inclusion in big-picture planning leaves multicultural agencies to work in a vacuum. While a clean slate is sometimes useful, it can also be counterproductive and inefficient in client-agency relationships, especially when clients are new to targeting multicultural consumers and want efforts to produce results and meet milestones. The absence of leadership involvement can lead to outcomes like these:

- The agency's market-research efforts might lack objective and respondent profile focus.
- White-space recommendations appropriate for a broad segment of multicultural consumers might seem like strong recommendations when, in fact, they are far removed from the brand's direction.

- The agency's marketing insights and recommendations might support category development when the company's goals are to develop the brand among existing category users.

Minimizing the Impact of the Disconnect

Clients who help their agencies understand their business and their marketing focus can prevent their agencies from veering off into unforeseen directions. For examples, agencies have been known to identify unmet needs and recommend unconventional products and services that would be at odds with the decision to target multicultural consumers because of their existing consumption behavior for a company's existing products and services.

When clients truly collaborate with their agencies, recommendations and execution are more creative and business relevant. For instance, agencies will more readily align with more relevant client activities and avoid canned promotions, sponsorships, and events tied to soccer, soap operas, and music festivals, which are not always relevant and are costly and short-lived or offer little differentiation, and the metrics may bear little or no relation to the KPIs the company is tracking and in which management is interested. Open communication also prevents the impact on agency morale when the client rejects a recommendation, which would unknowingly seem at odds with what the agency thinks the client wants from them. To minimize the impact of the communication divide, clients must do three things:

1. Inform their agencies of the products or services that represent the larger growth opportunity for the company and the types of consumers most likely to purchase their products and services
2. Inform their agencies that the company's attention and resources are laser focused and fully allocated to this larger opportunity
3. Instruct the agency that the multicultural target profile should match their existing customers

Clients must also be realistic about the time it will take to generate results. Building a brand takes time, money, and patience—especially when the brand is relatively unknown or when there is a brand leader in the category that has been targeting multicultural markets for many years. Continuity and sustainable efforts are the only way to build a brand, and clients should be realistic. Seemingly quick-hit opportunities do not exist and pressuring a multicultural agency to provide such solutions is unrealistic, disrespectful, and a huge morale buster.

On the other hand, clients must know better than to follow ill-conceived sure-hit agency recommendations to create new products, new distribution channels, and even entirely different businesses to capture a share of multicultural consumers' wallets. Companies have spent millions on such ill-advised ventures with unrealistic expectations for big results, but these examples are literally cases of the blind leading the blind. When the expected results don't occur, they shut down efforts and conclude that multicultural markets are not a viable investment. These efforts are inevitably short-lived because the financial and operational support dwindles when quick sales results don't materialize, especially considering different company priorities and investment focus.

Open communication is valuable on both sides. Clients are known to report that their multicultural agencies don't challenge their thinking or come to them with fresh and strategic solutions that align with the business. Ironically, clients often complain their multicultural agencies don't understand their business and attribute perceived deficiencies in performance to a lack of alignment with business goals and strategies. Clients must know that multicultural agencies will seldom make waves. Few want to risk losing the client's business by voicing concerns or opportunities for improvement. For this reason, it is important to invite open and regular dialogue with agency partners—not just once a year during the agency review. Agency management must have peer-to-peer dialogue with the company's C-suite and should expect to have their calls answered or returned rather than having a junior brand associate or multicultural manager with no authority or decision-making power leading the communication.

Internal Multicultural Experts

There has been a steady increase in the number of multicultural experts inside the halls of corporate America. Many companies have hired multicultural executives in marketing and sales positions to help them better understand multicultural consumers. On the surface, hiring multicultural marketing executives and creating multicultural departments appeared to be a promising step. Multicultural managers would be important liaisons within the client company and multicultural agencies. They would improve mutual understanding of business goals, strategies, and implementation direction, and they would ensure more aligned agency partnerships.

It seemed like the ideal solution. However, multicultural managers have only served to distance senior leadership even further from multicultural work and created the false impression that anything having to do with multicultural markets was somebody else's job. It has led the rest of the organization to disavow involvement with or responsibility for multicultural market activity, leaving multicultural managers in a position of having to constantly justify the value of multicultural markets and the value of their work.

Gloria Tostado has managed Fortune 500 marketing on the multicultural agency side, and she has managed multicultural market efforts for client companies such as BMO Harris Bank, Circuit City, and Verizon Wireless. During one of our conversations, she said, "Within companies with multicultural teams, the biggest challenge is the absence of accountability throughout the organization. Accountability for planning and implementation of multicultural work is limited to a handful of people—it is not recognized company wide."

Multicultural managers are often left to fend for themselves, and they are often as much in the dark about the company's big picture as are agency partners. They are seldom integrated into marketing's day-to-day objective setting, market research, planning meetings, strategy development, or implementation. Furthermore, they are seldom involved in planning and implementation conversations with functional and operational areas on which multicultural efforts depend to successfully deliver on a company's promise.

In a sense, little has changed. Multicultural managers must still work to develop relationships and introduce themselves quite literally into the company's marketing and operational activity to stay abreast of the work, to request participation in key meetings, and to request that functional areas like market research, advertising, public relations, and digital align implementation work to multicultural consumers—which is often rebutted for "lack of budget."

Despite the presence of multicultural managers, the integration of implementation work continues to be an afterthought. As a result, multicultural managers and the agencies they oversee are seldom able to impact strategic or implementation output, and they are often aligning to directions provided by general-market agencies. Discussions of marketing insights seldom take place with the voice of the multicultural consumer at the table. Strategies and implementation plans are often developed and shared with multicultural managers long after the window has closed for any multicultural insight to be considered or applied.

This internal dynamic has weakened the value of multicultural positions among those who hold them. As a result, these positions have long been considered dead-end jobs among executives on a fast track, and they do not easily attract top talent. When they do, individuals quickly feel the stigma of being associated with multicultural work.

Fearful that their careers will stagnate, multicultural managers ask to be transferred out of multicultural responsibilities as quickly as possible because this is the only way to receive the exposure, recognition, and advancement that matter to their careers. When these lateral or upward moves are not available to them, they leave their companies within eighteen to twenty-four months, feeling disheartened, unaccomplished, and exhausted.

Three basic problems need to be addressed for multicultural managers and departments to deliver on the value and potential of multicultural markets:

Problem 1: Multicultural departments are treated as silos in the same way as the multicultural agencies they oversee. Neither they nor their input is integrated in day-to-day business management and operational discussions. **Solution:** Targeting multicultural consumers must become a core competency for those who manage overall strategy development and implementation. While there can be internal experts, those with the power to impact the business must be accountable for the company-wide integration of and support for multicultural market focus planning and implementation.

Problem 2: Multicultural managers do not have decision-making power and, consequently, cannot impact the business. Their work is reactive rather than proactive. They follow instead of walk in step with the company's strategic and marketing direction. **Solution:** Strategy expansion into multicultural markets must be led and overseen by a senior leader who can impact the business.

Problem 3: Multicultural managers are given a limited budget or no budget at all. They depend on their ability to convince those with a budget on the value of their recommendations to generate multicultural market sales. As one multicultural manager put it, "We typically have to tin-cup for money and beg for functional and operational support. When support is given, it is often given begrudgingly." **Solution:** Strategy-expansion budgets and cross functional responsibility for integrating multicultural targets must be clear to stakeholders and must be integrated into operational implementation plans.

The Consolidation of Multicultural Marketing

The multicultural market continues to grow largely because of natural births in the United States and, to a lesser extent, because of immigration. There is a large and growing millennial multicultural generation, which is mostly U.S. born and English speaking. Many multicultural adults whose first language is other than English speak at least some English and have lived in the country for many years.

As multicultural markets evolve, generational, linguistic, and cultural insights are increasingly controversial, complex, and, at times, convenient excuses for undifferentiated efforts. On the surface, recent demographic, generational, and cultural trends might imply that multicultural implementation efforts are no different than implementation for non-Hispanic white consumers—in English and with the same messages and approaches. But adopting this mind-set is wrong and is often the result of selective reasoning. Two examples of this selective reasoning have been particularly controversial—consolidation of multicultural agency work at general-market agencies and dissolution of multicultural marketing units. We'll look at each in turn.

First, marketers have been consolidating their advertising work among fewer and fewer creative and media agencies to create efficiencies for many years. However, marketers should use caution not to misunderstand superficial interpretations of multicultural market data and rely on them to consolidate multicultural agency work at general-market agencies. Client companies—including Home Depot, Burger King, and El Pollo Loco, to name a few—began this consolidation trend in 2010. Burger King said that its multicultural customers had evolved to be younger English-speaking consumers. Home Depot cited the desire to achieve a consistent voice, and El Pollo Loco said it wanted to ensure that multicultural work moved in step with overall marketing efforts. These are logical reasons, but all could have been achieved without consolidation and with the senior client involvement and agency communication. The irony is that most general-market agencies do not have a good history with multicultural work. They have demonstrated neither expertise nor interest in multicultural work or in the allocation of people or budget resources to target them—not to mention a vehement resistance to the allocation of client budgets away from work that targets nonmulticultural consumers.

Some years ago, I was hired by Chiat/Day Advertising to join their account-planning department. Along with my general-market planning duties for five of the eleven Nissan regions in the United States, my planner colleagues and I were also assigned "niche" market responsibilities for the African American, college, military, and Hispanic markets. We were asked to think about how to grow these niche markets for our Nissan client. Being Hispanic, I was assigned the Hispanic niche. With no prior experience in Hispanic marketing, I called upon the Spanish-language media to support me with data for my due-diligence analysis. Soon after, I was presenting a business case to Nissan USA and asking for a budget for a branding campaign to launch one of Nissan's newly designed compact models in Miami and Los Angeles in Spanish.

To my surprise, Nissan approved the proposed budget. When dealership owners in other regions found out, I was asked by Chiat's regional offices (eleven nationally) to present the opportunity to several dealer groups across the country. The dealers were excited about the prospect of supporting Nissan sales among Hispanics in their regions, and they started to pressure Chiat to develop regional Spanish-language advertising support for their markets.

I thought I was successfully carrying out my duties. However, this view was not shared by Chiat's management. They were not only upset about Nissan's allocation of budget to the Hispanic niche, which they saw as taking away from further allocation to general-market budget to launch that same model, but also upset about the time I was dedicating to the Hispanic segment because of the shower of requests coming in from the regions. I was told in no uncertain terms that I had created a monster and that I had to make it go away. I was told I'd been hired as a planner for general-market work, not to focus on Hispanic market work.

After Chiat/Day, I joined a Hispanic agency start-up where I ultimately became managing partner and VP of account services. For over eight years, I managed the marketing campaigns for an impressive list of Fortune 500 clients. On many occasions during this time, I was asked to collaborate with several of our clients' agencies of record. My experience collaborating with general-market agencies was fraught with indifference, arrogance, and fierce competitiveness.

This firsthand experience with general-market agencies' resistance to thinking, planning, and investing in multicultural marketing left little room for optimism that things have changed for the better. This said, a shift has been taking place. Several large general-market agencies have launched multicultural spin-offs devoted to specific multicultural segments to compete directly with multicultural agencies.

The downside is that as general-market agencies hire multicultural executives, they become token hires. They can seldom add value or have the power to impact the work. They report being hired to be seen and not heard unless they are specifically asked to do so. They are figureheads who are brought to client meetings so the agency can claim multicultural expertise and gain credibility to bring those budgets in-house. These individuals feel undervalued and are treated similarly to client-side multicultural managers. Ironically, multicultural executives hired for account services or creative positions at large general market agencies initially feel proud to be hired, but once disenchantment sets in, they use their "big agency" work experience to update their résumés to leave their unrewarding experiences behind.

General-market agencies have also been acquiring multicultural agencies to quickly gain necessary resources and credibility. However, as with most acquisitions where the culture is what fuels creativity and differentiation, the need to conform to general-market criteria leads these acquisitions to quickly lose their fire. Acquired multicultural agencies soon regret having to sacrifice the integrity of their work as it goes through general-market filters and criteria. Similar frustrations are felt among multicultural agencies when clients assign oversight responsibility for multicultural agency work to their general-market agencies, in many cases results in dictates to adapt general-market creative to target multicultural consumers. In principle, this is not necessarily wrong if the right insights are considered in the concepts, but in-house multicultural agencies often face resistance to this type of input.

Clients should consider the impact of placing agency personnel and their multicultural agencies in these highly charged positions because it seldom bodes well for inspired and effective creativity that generates the desired response among multicultural consumers.

The second action marketers like Walmart, McDonald's, Nestlé, H&R Block, and others have started taking is reorganizing multicultural responsibilities. Companies began assigning responsibility for multicultural work to respective brand groups and business units with the intent to integrate multicultural responsibilities under each business owner's leadership. This direction has merit because it moves companies closer to the integrated implementation approach, of which I am a proponent. However, it's important to recognize that given the current lack of knowledge, lack of comfort, and lack of a clearly defined strategy-expansion approach, forced overnight integration is unlikely to be successful.

Multicultural marketing has mostly been considered someone else's responsibility. At best, it has been managed at arm's length; at worst, it's been an externally focused and managed activity. It's a hot potato that, without proper planning, training, and defined accountability, few are eager to catch. Marketers and cross-functional managers cannot be expected to wake up one day and be culturally, psychologically, and emotionally competent or even ready and willing to think through and manage this responsibility. To effectively integrate multicultural talent and benefit from the value of doing so, leaders must be willing to do the following:

- Reposition multicultural efforts within the organization as a new strategic expansion
- Provide a clear business case with KPIs that align with the total business
- Appoint C-level leadership
- Allocate budgets commensurate with the task
- Communicate clear roles and ensure access and visibility of multicultural experts within the organization
- Enforce a mechanism that holds decision makers responsible and accountable for integrated performance
- Lead a transformation that enables cultural competency and effective consumer targeting irrespective of cultural background

Total Market Relevance

As companies began to dissolve their multicultural groups and reassign the work of multicultural agencies, the Association of National Advertisers (ANA) started speaking of the concept of "total market," and this concept has become a strong catalyst for the agency and client-side consolidation and integration.

The intent of the total-market concept was to convey the ever-growing importance of integrating multicultural consumer insights into clients' marketing processes and budgets because multicultural consumers have become such a sizable proportion of the country's consumer population. The premise of a total market is very valid. Ten years ago, I wrote about it in my book *Marketing to Hispanics: A Strategic Approach to Assessing and Planning Your Initiative*, except I referred to it as integration.

Given the ANA's focus on advertising, there is a crucial difference in scope between the ANA's definition and my own. The ANA defines *total market* within the context of marketing.

When I speak of *integration*, I'm talking about its application across the business enterprise. I'm referring to company processes and functions, including marketing. A company's business-model effectiveness depends on all its components working toward company goals—not just the marketing component. As such, the role of all components must be considered when integrating multicultural consumer insights. It's going to take more than interesting business frameworks or terms to enable marketers to integrate and implement with multicultural relevance.

No matter what we call it, whether total market or integration, for these frameworks to truly work in clients' favor, companies must be willing and able to approach targeting multicultural consumers methodically and with conviction. For this to happen, marketers must first define the value and rewards to their business and then organize their businesses to implement relevantly—or risk being challenged by unproductive management models, internal indifference, irrelevant resource allocation, and unproductive outcomes.

This chapter has addressed the many challenges experienced by both marketers and their multicultural agencies going back thirty years, and many of them are as relevant today as they ever were. Marketers and their agencies are caught in a vicious cycle as they test novel approaches to successfully grow their sales by targeting multicultural consumers. I believe it's safe to say that they haven't even scratched the surface of their potential.

There is an important opportunity for companies to broaden their view of the country's consumer population, to increase their knowledge of the cultures represented among consumers, and to develop a greater appreciation of consumers who are different from themselves. Client companies must challenge themselves to evolve so they can see and appreciate people of other cultures as three-dimensional human beings who make buying decisions rather than two-dimensional data points on reports and presentations. As we discussed in Chapter 1, the United States has changed forever. Leadership must help their organizations adapt to this change. They must help them develop the necessary cultural intelligence to make business relevant decisions that are not clouded by personal bias, hesitation, or fear.

I often say to my clients that *we tend to do well by the people we take the time to get to know, and we don't do so well by those we know nothing about.* Companies need to take the time to get to know all consumers with the potential to buy their products. Companies need to demonstrate that they understand and appreciate their multicultural targets. When companies get this right, multicultural consumers will reward them with their wallets. They will become champions for their brands, and companies will accelerate revenue growth beyond the imaginable. It's simple. If companies develop the business sense, capabilities, cultural competency, and heart to effectively implement their strategies in multicultural markets, the right internal and agency model will be self-evident, and they will maximize growth goals in their expansion to multicultural markets.

Think of it this way: economists and the business community have been saying that the country's workforce needs to step up its skills so workers and companies can benefit from the growing pool of new economy jobs.

The same can be said about our companies' ability to benefit from the large and growing pool of multicultural consumers. But companies must also step up their knowledge, appreciation, and capabilities to benefit from the increased revenue potential they represent.

What's Your Strategy?

Experience has taught many companies that just "doing something" to target multicultural consumers is a bad investment and will not be productive. This experience has led many companies to give up altogether. But much of the confusion, lack of commitment, arbitrary resource allocations, and the vicious cycle companies experience in their attempts to target multicultural consumers stem from not being clear about the reasons for targeting this consumer base in the first place and how this market fits within the company's growth strategy.

Every company has a growth strategy comprising of strategic platforms its leaders believe will give it a position of competitive advantage to generate robust growth. These platforms often include product leadership though innovation, market development or brand penetration, customer experience, operational excellence, and so forth. Strategies on which most companies focus and against which company resources are allocated are driven by the business model and those opportunities that can accelerate growth in the short term. However, most smart companies also have midterm and long-term strategies intended to capture opportunities that will help the company remain competitive over time. This may entail consideration of near-future growth possibilities where their strategies could be leveraged in diverse ways or in different markets.

Midterm strategies could include expanding a company's existing strategy into new consumer markets or into new geographies. These could also include creating new divisions or new product lines. White-space projects fall into this strategy category. These are efforts where the new market and geographies exist or where new business lines can be quickly researched and developed. Once these opportunities are uncovered, it's just a matter of organizing a leadership team and allocating the necessary resources to successfully expand into these areas within one to three years.

Companies also engage in long-term strategies that could include investments in emerging technologies, emerging companies, and R&D projects to explore possibilities, à la Jeff Bezos and Elon Musk. These types of projects may or may not come to fruition, require significant investment over time, and have lengthy development time frames but are necessary investments for future growth.

Targeting multicultural consumers is a midterm strategy. It is meant to expand a company's existing strategy into a new consumer market. It should focus on identifying and targeting multicultural consumers who already use or have the propensity to buy a company's products and services. Targeting multicultural consumers could be defined as a white-space market gap with the potential to generate revenue growth. The goal for this strategy should be brand penetration of existing products and services, not market, product, or service development. As such, a multicultural market expansion effort should be based on the company's existing business and marketing strategies.

It is necessary to ensure that the delivery of the company's existing strategies is relevant and accessible to its targeted multicultural consumers. The focus should be on how the company will generate sales and market-share growth and on how the company needs to organize to develop its internal capabilities to capture growth in this new target market. These capabilities will be required in every part of the organization that is currently focused on the short-term strategy implementation.

Chapter 5

The Necessary Paradigm

The old rules for doing business are serving us less and less; in many ways, they've become obsolete. Similarly, the models and frameworks used to target multicultural consumers continue to be unproductive. The vicious cycle of failed attempts discussed in earlier chapters reminds me of the Albert Einstein quote "Insanity is doing the same thing repeatedly and expecting different results."

We need to adopt a paradigm that more effectively helps to reframe the growing economic value multicultural consumers offer U.S. businesses. In the 1999 book *Alchemy of Growth*, Mehrdad Baghai, Stephen Coley, and David White, long-time McKinsey consultants, talk about the Three Horizons Framework. This framework is a time-honored planning structure used by many successful businesses, and it makes great sense for companies looking for new revenue streams with future growth potential.

This framework proposes that a company should engage in growth based on three time and profit horizons: Horizon One, Horizon Two, and Horizon Three. As the authors point out, Horizon One focuses on immediate-term profits and cash flow. The emphasis is on implementing aspects of the strategy that protect the core business, improve performance, and maximize value for the company. This focus requires the greatest investment because it is the revenue engine of the business.

Horizon Two focuses on growth opportunities in the near term, or the focus is on identifying new sources of revenue and market-share growth with the potential to generate significant profits in two to three years. Sources of growth could be new geographies or new consumer groups to which the company could expand its strategies by leveraging current strengths and assets and by adapting to the needs in the new geography or among the new consumer group. This activity requires moderate investment, but the potential to contribute a significant and growing proportion of the company's future revenue is high.

Horizon Three activity focuses on longer-term growth. It focuses on ideas for growth in five to ten years. This activity might include initiatives such as R&D projects, test programs, or minority ownership in new businesses.

Baghai, Coley, and White propose that "to ensure growth into the future, companies need to engage in and manage all three growth horizons concurrently, albeit with proportionately appropriate management and investment focus. On average, 70 percent of management's focus should be on Horizon One—profits, ROI, and cash flow. Twenty percent of management's focus and resources should be allocated to developing Horizon Two growth—identifying and gaining a position of advantage in a geography or among new consumer groups with a focus on revenue, market share, and net present value (NPV). And ten percent of the company's focus and resources should be directed to Horizon Three investments— creating and investing in viable ideas and options for the future."

Targeting multicultural consumers in the United States must be recognized as a Horizon Two activity. It represents a growth strategy that will enable U.S. companies to grow revenue and market share within one to three years given the proper focus and investment of resources, and "it has the potential to contribute a significant and growing proportion of the company's future revenue."

As discussed in Chapters 1 and 2, the significant size and expected continued growth of multicultural populations, their enormous spending power, and their strong consumption behavior on myriad categories represent robust growth potential for U.S. companies for the foreseeable future. U.S. companies must reframe their view of the market from one that deserves only isolated focus and investment to one with a specific strategic purpose—new growth that is aligned with their existing growth strategies and that is implemented to gain positions of advantage in the multicultural market into the future.

This is significant because gaining a position of advantage in this growth market is crucial to building shareholder value. Historically, the market rewards competitive advantages in new markets with a higher PE ratio based on expected future performance. Today's whirlwind of demographic and cultural change requires that companies pay attention and move quickly to reframe the value of multicultural targets as a critical source of growth. Pursuing Horizon Two activity requires shifting gears to meet implementation requirements.

Internal Resistance to Change

Few people like or welcome change, and we like it even less when the change is related to something with which we have little familiarity and experience. Some marketers would rather avoid or downplay a new consumer-group opportunity because it seems complex or different and implies change. This is especially true amid Horizon One priorities that require a person's full mastery of his or her work. People usually want to feel in control of their realm of expertise, and marketers are no different. They fear appearing uncertain or incompetent about a new market. And they certainly don't like new and unfamiliar endeavors that require them to reallocate budgets and take risks.

The unfamiliar has a way of threatening the confidence of even the most experienced marketer, meaning there is resistance to new and unfamiliar customer groups. Some resist understanding how to engage them, and they resist investing to improve strategy delivery. Alternatively, they move slowly and cautiously, and they rationalize that it makes the most sense to make just a few adjustments until results can be seen. Others rationalize it's best to make only those adjustments that are critical. I often wonder on what criteria these "cautious" and "critical" adjustments are based. In the absence of any fact-based criteria, these statements tend to be rationalizations for doing and investing as few resources as possible.

Think about what would happen if, in the normal course of business, you observed a decision maker who seemed uncertain about the value of a new customer group's contributions to business growth and unsure of how to capture their business. Imagine that he or she is hesitant about taking the necessary steps to grow this new business. Many decision makers behave in this manner when faced with the opportunity to generate business from new multicultural consumer groups. It isn't that they don't see the opportunity. It's that they're not going to take risks if they haven't been given a mandate from the top to do so—a mandate that comes with measures of accountability and a budget to make it happen.

A highly successful middle manager for a multinational CPG company with 2017 gross sales of $89 billion who came from Mexico to run the multicultural business told me that her biggest frustration in her position is the task of having to always be selling and trying to convince brand managers on the value of investing in growing the company's brands among U.S. Hispanics. She said that despite clear volume and share trends that show that Hispanics are driving business growth for the company's brands, many of the brand managers remain lukewarm about growing their investments in the Hispanic market because they are fearful of how this might impact the "core" business.

Protecting the core business—a Horizon One activity—should be a priority for these managers. It is the single most important source of profits, ROI, and cash flow—in the short term. However, there is value in not losing sight of new market opportunities that represent future growth activity—Horizon Two. Multinational companies know this well. After all, this is how they became multinational companies.

According to this executive, fear of failure, including damaged reputation and missed promotions, drives the current behavior within this organization. It's easy to see the predicament. These managers are being held accountable for producing short-term results and are rewarded for growing and defending the brands' market share. They are not accountable or being rewarded for growing a new consumer market—Horizon Two activity. It makes sense that all their attention and decisions for resource allocations will be directed toward their focal point, no matter how attractive another market may seem. To successfully capture new business among new consumer groups, those assigned the work must understand how and where it fits strategically for the company, business unit, or brand group. How it fits within their brand-implementation plans and within their budgets must be clear. And most importantly, how they will be held accountable and rewarded must be clear.

Ironically, there were plans underway to dissolve the multicultural unit at her company, thereby making each brand manager responsible for multicultural consumers at their discretion. The multicultural staff she once managed would be reassigned to specific brand groups to provide multicultural expertise as needed. This manager returned to Mexico to run a large division for the same company, feeling skeptical that the planned reorganization would succeed.

External Resistance to Change

Companies sometimes experience what they call "backlash" from customers who don't like the idea of U.S. companies adjusting their businesses to meet the needs of customers from diverse backgrounds. It typically originates from older populations with more nationalist and conservative views.

Experiences with backlash are growing less frequent, especially in markets with larger multicultural populations. Yet companies often retreat when they receive letters and emails expressing disapproval of bilingual or other efforts that target specific ethnicities. Companies are rightly concerned about upsetting their core customers. Oftentimes employees aren't prepared to respond to these types of complaints, leaving them speechless or prompting them to apologize. Neither of these responses bodes well for the company.

The right solution is to assess where the company stands regarding its values and to proactively communicate this throughout the organization, including providing a company statement that employees can use when customers voice their concern. Most clients reference the company's commitment to serve the needs of all its customers in the diverse communities they serve.

To be fair, taking a stand requires courage and conviction for which not all companies are prepared, especially when social tension is heightened. For instance, after the 2016 elections and throughout 2017, companies appeared to hit the pause button in their efforts to visibly invest in growing their multicultural business, especially among Hispanics.

The nation is experiencing a period of marked hostility and uncertainty. Nationalism and nativism are at an all-time high. The government maintains an anti-immigrant stance, often depicting immigrants as a security threat to the nation. There have been several attempts to enforce a travel ban. Deportation threats and border security—the wall—are highly charged topics. Immigration reform is an even more contentious and heated topic and was exacerbated by the announcement to repeal the Deferred Action for Childhood Arrivals Act (DACA—Dreamers Act), which remains fraught with uncertainty and has become a negotiation chip to gain support for other concessions. To avoid backlash from supporters of the current administration, companies significantly reduced or withdrew their multicultural investments. Over the course of 2017, anti-immigrant sentiment and the recoiling from the multicultural marketplace by businesses drove declines in immediate foot traffic and sales volume for many brands and retailers, generating significant concerns among businesses.

At the same time, more than eight hundred Fortune 500 CEOs—including Apple CEO Tim Cook, Microsoft CEO Satya Nadella, Amazon CEO Jeff Bezos, Google CEO Sundar Pichai, Uber CTO Thuan Pham, Airbnb CEO Brian Chesky, and prominent individuals such as Warren Buffett—saw value in stepping up and advocating for the Dreamers in a letter dated September 20, 2017. The letter was addressed to House Speaker Paul Ryan, House Minority Leader Nancy Pelosi, Senate Majority Leader Mitch McConnell, and Senate Minority Leader Charles E. Schumer.

The letter says, "DACA recipients grew up in America, registered with the government, submitted to extensive background checks, and are diligently giving back to their communities and paying income taxes. More than 97 percent are in school or in the workforce, 5 percent started their own business, 65 percent have purchased a vehicle, and 16 percent have purchased their first home."

Many of these companies publicly pledged the necessary legal investments to protect their DACA employees from being deported. The letter further argued that the U.S. economy would lose $460.3 billion from the national GDP and $24.6 billion in social security and Medicare tax contributions from Dreamers and emphasized that at least 72 percent of the top twenty-five Fortune 500 companies counted DACA recipients among their employees. They stressed that Dreamers are vital to the future of their companies and the economy, saying "with them, we grow and create jobs. They are part of why we will continue to have a global competitive advantage."

Rethinking the "Core" Market

Companies concerned about protecting their core markets and making sure they don't upset them often don't realize or may choose to ignore how significantly their core markets have changed. Protecting the core market is the number-one source of resistance to reallocating budgets to capture high-value multicultural targets. This is because most middle managers are compensated to focus on Horizon One activities, which emphasize protecting core-market share and short-term gains.

However, other factors also contribute to the struggle managers face, including outdated views of today's consumer market and, to some extent, denial and resistance to accepting the country's demographic realities. While we all see the manifestation of this demographic change through the plethora of ethnic food choices, the music we listen to, and even the way we speak and shop, marketers otherwise turn a blind eye to the presence of large and growing populations who are also potential customers. Interestingly, some marketers may think this is a new phenomenon and don't realize or choose to ignore that the multicultural population has lived in the United States for generations and already include the core customers they are trying to protect, albeit with some culture-based beliefs and behaviors.

In 2010, Peter Francese, the founder of *American Demographics* magazine, explained that "the concept of an 'average American' is gone and probably forever." Francese reported that "U.S. households have grown ever more complex and varied such that describing or marketing to the 'average American' is no longer a relevant undertaking."

Consider the following statistics provided by Francese, which speak to the absence of the "average consumer":

- **We are a multisegmented household economy.** No single household type describes even one-third of U.S. households. The once typical notion of males as heads of household is upended by the fact that most heads of household are female, and a very large proportion of heads of household are grandparents. The iconic family with a dad, mom, and kids represents fewer than one-fifth of all households.

- **We are a multicultural nation.** The country is increasingly multicultural, and over three hundred of the country's largest counties have majority minority populations. The U.S. Hispanic population is the largest minority segment and is growing at a dramatic rate. Ethnic plurality, which has already occurred in the most populous states, has also occurred among the U.S. baby population and is scheduled to happen among children under age eighteen by 2020.

- **We are a multigenerational society.** There is a large younger population and a large older population. Almost half of Gen Z, Y, and X are multicultural, while 60 to 78 percent of boomer and senior generations are non-Hispanic white. Culturally, young and old are quite distinct not only because of their age but also because of the multicultural influence on younger generations and lack thereof among the older.

These facts make it clear that today's definition of a core market is rooted in the "utopian fifties" and is highly distorted.

In 2017, seven years after the 2010 census, the multisegmented economies as well as the multigenerational and multicultural mix Francese described in 2010 is even more pronounced and requires that companies think more broadly about their core market. In the new paradigm, Horizon One core-market activity should be protected, but there must also be a recognition that this core market has changed and will continue to change and there are implications to continuing to market to the average consumer. Companies must be able to see beyond race and ethnicity. They must be able to more broadly identify customer profiles with the greatest propensity to buy their company's products and services, regardless of age, gender, or ethnic and cultural identity.

This paradigm shift requires that companies rethink the profile of consumers already contributing to their revenue streams as well as those who can potentially contribute to existing and new revenue streams. It also requires relevant delivery of their strategies. As Francese said during our conversation, "If you want to be the choice of a new consumer generation, it is critical to embrace the cultures and voices of that generation."

High-Value Targets

For some leaders, the thought of becoming familiar with multicultural consumers is overwhelming. After all, there are so many of them, from so many different countries, and they speak so many different languages and dialects. But in fact, it's very simple.

It is not necessary for every company or every brand to become familiar with all multicultural consumers' wants and needs. The good news is you only need to do the work to become familiar with those segments of multicultural populations that are high-value customers for your brands. More good news: you already know the characteristics of your brands' high-value targets, so the work ahead only requires you to identify those same characteristics among multicultural populations in the markets where you do business and then organize to expand the delivery of your current strategies to these segments—Horizon Two activity.

The time may come when you decide to expand beyond these high-value targets. In time, it may make sense to add a secondary target because there is future value in investing to develop your category and brand among consumers who don't currently use your products or brand. This takes significant and longer-term investment. Or the company may determine it can make its products and services more relevant to introduce new consumers to its brands. However, these are white-space endeavors and not where most companies should begin. When a company is just getting started or if existing efforts are being recalibrated, the focus should be on the consumer profiles among whom its category is already well-developed; the goals should be improving brand position—market-share gains.

To define your high-value multicultural targets, only two questions must be answered.

- How is your company planning to grow this year? What are its growth strategies?

- On which products and services is your company planning to focus? What are its focus growth platforms—products, divisions, or geographies?

The answers to these questions will help define the profile of the high-value multicultural targets on which to focus the company's Horizon Two activity. Relevant delivery of your strategy should focus on those areas that are crucial to sales generation and retention, including:

- Organizational Structure
- Infrastructure
- Retail Operations
- Employees
- Products and Services
- Marketing
- Digital

For example, if your company sells life insurance, your high-value targets might be males between the age of twenty-five and fifty-four with a household income of $50,000 or higher. Among multicultural consumers, they could be both foreign or U.S. born. They will have established households and own assets like a house. They will have kids, perhaps kids in college or kids they'd like to send to college, and they might own a small business. They will likely speak at least some English, but they may prefer to discuss insurance issues and decisions in Spanish or their native language.

Relevant expansion and delivery of a strategy to attract them could include ensuring that all company communication is bilingual. This would include the company's website, the newsletter, letters, premium statements, notices, and product brochures. It may be important to make some slight modifications to the company's message to address the target's values, beliefs, attitudes, and misconceptions about the value of life insurance. Technology infrastructure would need to be programmed to produce bilingual letters, notices, and statements and to capture and report on sales of multicultural policies.

Voice response unit (VRU) systems would need to be set up so the main message provides an in-language prompt to press a determined number to be redirected within the first ten seconds. This small action minimizes dropped call rates by over 50 percent. Perhaps a second toll-free number can be established to provide direct connection to the Spanish-certified bilingual call team and appropriate on-hold messages and instructions in Spanish recorded for that line. If only one toll-free number is used, the VRU system would be programmed so language-of-origin calls can be directed to the appropriate bilingual representative without falling out of the language tree. Recorded messages that are played after the caller switches language would need to be recorded in the caller's language of choice.

Several claims-and-benefits customer-service representatives would need to be bilingual, and their on-screen scripts would need to be adapted and translated. Customer representatives would be trained on the targets' values, beliefs, attitudes, and misconceptions about the value of life insurance. Call metrics would need to be modified to account for lengthier conversations and longer call times when they occur in the customer's language of origin.

Insurance sales agents could be bilingual or English speaking, but they would go through cultural-awareness and cultural-competency training. Relationships would need to be formed with community organizations, and any efforts to present life-insurance benefits at community meetings would need to be bilingual.

Defining the company's high-value target profile is a crucial step in minimizing confusion about multicultural markets, their specific needs and requirements, and necessary optimization work to be done on the company's operations and infrastructure.

Getting to Know Them

Once you define your high-value multicultural target profile, it's important to implement the same type of market research typically conducted on the rest of your high-value targets, preferably as part of the same studies. The goal should be to get to know these targets to the same degree as you know the rest of your core-target consumers. It's important that this research analysis and insights development be conducted in close collaboration with the market-research company.

Hire a market-research company experienced in multicultural research because there are differences in the way survey instruments are developed for diverse cultural groups. It's also important that the research company be experienced with the culture being researched so they have context for and can explain the behavior reflected in the research.

I advise and support several multinational market-research companies with their Hispanic studies because their internal analysts do not always have sufficient understanding of the Hispanic culture as it pertains to their attitudes and usage of a variety of product and service categories. This means they can't explain the cultural contexts behind the findings, and often response patterns that veer away from the familiar are reported as unusual behavior or can't be explained at all. You can find a list of qualified companies in the references section.

The main questions to answer once the target is defined include the following:

- How large is the multicultural user base for my brand?
- How large is it as a proportion of my total target?
- What is their purchase propensity compared to the rest of the target?
- What proportion of my sales do they represent?
- What is the sales potential they represent to our brands?
- Why aren't they buying our brand? For example, are they simply not engaged with our category and not buying our product—life insurance—or are they buying it from a competitor?

Depending on your industry, a subscription to syndicated data from companies like Simmons, Spectra, Scarborough, Nielsen, IRI, and a host of industry-specific providers can help answer the first two questions. Your company may already subscribe to syndicated data; if so, you can ask if they provide specific reads on multicultural segments and obtain it in a way that makes comparing easy. If they don't provide specific reads, ask how they can accommodate your needs.

Internal sales data is also valuable. When sales data is not yet readable by target segments, it can be analyzed by geography and cultural segment concentration. Companies like Geoscape, which combines geographically coded sales data with cultural segments to determine where and among which target segments the opportunity is greatest and growing fastest, provides this kind of analysis. This exercise can be done for the overall target as well for Hispanic, Asian, and African American consumers.

Other options are available too. It is possible to obtain a fully compiled report using the syndicated data sources mentioned earlier from companies like marketresearch.com and Packaged Facts. For $2,000 to $3,000, they compile and analyze data using industry and government sources for a variety of industries. This is a cost-efficient way to obtain a high-level comprehensive read of your industry based on multicultural consumers. Large media outlets can also provide market sizing, usage, and attitudes analysis on request if they view you as a good advertising prospect. Just make sure to be very specific about the questions you're trying to answer and the data format that will best serve your analysis.

Once you have a big-picture view, specific questions will undoubtedly surface. These questions will be the basis for a proprietary study. If the questions are few and straightforward, companies like ThinkNow Research, GfK, and ORC International offer cost-efficient omnibus products. It's possible to buy open-and closed-ended questions to help answer specific issues. This option is usually best for categories where the target is broad because, as you may already know, omnibus studies are typically conducted in set markets and among a set profile of respondents. Any alterations, although possible, will raise the cost. If the alterations are many, then a proprietary study may be the best approach.

Once you have a solid understanding of market size and usage dynamics, you may find that there are proportions of your target who don't buy your brand or shop in your locations. Qualitative research is the only way to find out why targets who are highly engaged with a category are not buying a brand. Market-immersion experiences are the best approach to gain an understanding and appreciation for these insights. Not only will immersive work get you close to the target, but also, you'll see how they shop for your category firsthand and why they choose the way they do.

Many of my clients spend one or two days in markets where their targets live and shop. They're able to experience the target in their environment and gain an appreciation for who they are as people and as consumers. Often we engage targets in conversation; we listen to their stories, their journeys, and their perceptions of the companies where they do business as well as their motivations as consumers. It's always a revealing and life-changing experience for clients who allow themselves to be immersed in these types of experiences.

How quickly multicultural consumer choices are swayed will also depend on what your competition is already doing to capture these sales and how long they've been at work. It will also depend on how well and how quickly your company can match or exceed competitive offerings beyond the customer experiences the competition provides—without going off your strategy.

This last part is important. Many companies do a good job sizing the opportunity and understanding consumers' behaviors and attitudes but fall short when it comes to organizing internally to deliver on a seamless and frictionless customer experience, which is the most important aspect of implementing a strategy. This lack of alignment and resistant internal support has mostly to do with a lack of clarity as to the goals a company may have and the resources it is prepared to invest to expand its strategy into a new market—the U.S. multicultural market.

Even though the U.S. multicultural market is a domestic market, targeting it for the first time successfully is a Horizon Two activity. It is a midterm growth strategy. Interested companies must educate their people on the task and align people, resources, metrics, accountability, and rewards accordingly. Success won't come when efforts are left to the discretion of the manager who catches the multicultural hot potato on any given day.

Chapter 6

Organizing for Success

Like any important growth initiative worth pursuing, successfully expanding a strategy into a new market requires a comprehensive set of changes. And as discussed in Chapters 3 and 4, numerous improvement opportunities exist among companies currently wanting to grow sales or clients' sales by tapping multicultural consumers. To maximize the extraordinary economic potential of multicultural markets, cultural alignment must exist. Side by side, strategy and corporate culture are vital levers that ensure the viability and effectiveness of any growth endeavor.

Strategy provides clarity and focus for decisions and collective action. Implementation plans and options move people toward required action and are enforced through accountability measures, rewards for reaching goals, and consequences for failure to do so. Strategy also considers external environment assessments that warn when changes like strategy expansions are required for continued growth.

Corporate culture, while a softer and more elusive lever, is critical for attaining desired performance. When the values, beliefs, mind-sets, and behavior of leaders and employees don't align with the goals of a strategy, performance will suffer despite detailed and thoughtful plans. As Peter Drucker once said, culture eats strategy for lunch.

Shifting Mind-Sets and Culture

A shift in mind-set and corporate culture can only begin and be effective with a visible enlightenment and commitment in the C-suite. The C-suite must assert its full appreciation and understanding of the country's demographic changes and inextricably link this change to the company's ability to meet performance and build shareholder value goals into the future. To successfully expand a company's business strategy to the U.S. multicultural market, the company's appreciation for diverse markets not only globally but also domestically must be declared. This shift requires top-level leadership to model and enforce the company's strategic and cultural focus.

Of course, this is easier said than done. Mind-sets are shaped by a lifetime of experiences, and many people employed in corporate America, especially older generations, lack interaction and experiences with diverse populations. To change mind-sets and corporate culture requires education that builds cultural awareness and cultural competency.

For an organization's leadership and its employees to adopt a broader view of the U.S. consumer market and potential employees, it must learn about and experience a diverse set of people firsthand, not just in presentations or through online course modules but up close and personal, outside—in the neighborhoods, on the streets, in places of worship, and, if possible, in their homes. This isn't just an exercise for the research department; culture education must include top decision makers. Top leadership must become comfortable and even excited about the company's possibilities of developing reciprocal relationships with new markets and the company's brands.

Think of it as an adventure. Many decision makers are lucky enough to travel to distant countries where they experience people of other cultures, their history, their customs, their food, their music, their museums, and their families. Culture exploration in our own country can be just as exciting; 75.6 million international tourists visited the United States in 2016. They were drawn to the diverse cultural experiences found in many of the country's ethnic neighborhoods just as much as they were to Disney World, the Statue of Liberty, or the Golden Gate Bridge.

As the demographic makeup of the population continues evolving, cultural awareness and cultural competency will represent a tremendous competitive strength. It will enable the organization to easily recognize how to adapt the implementation of its strategy to make its brand more attractive to a broader set of consumers. Organizing for success is a process. It will happen in pace with top leadership's ability to understand and respond to cultural differences, to mobilize the organization in ways that are relevant to new targets, and, more importantly, to tie rewards and consequences to performance.

The Customer-Centric Myth

Being customer centric has been a catchphrase for many years and describes a company that manages its business to create positive consumer experiences consistently across all the points where the consumer engages with the company. This way of doing business builds value for a company because it differentiates it from the competition and makes the company more attractive to consumers.

Many companies aim to be customer centric but fall short in delivering a consistently positive customer experience, especially to culturally diverse customers. This is a problem that costs companies an estimated $100 billion annually in lost purchases and defections to the competition. Consider that many of those defecting may be multicultural consumers who control $3.5 trillion in spending power.

This is a shortcoming for many companies, but it's unfair to blame them for not knowing how to be relevant to multicultural consumers, especially when everything looks like it's supposed to from their perspective. This is where cultural awareness and cultural competency become extremely valuable. In his white paper "The Six Laws of Customer Experience," Bruce Temkin, managing partner of the Temkin Group, notes, "Given most people want their company to better serve customers, a clear view of what customers need, want, and dislike can align decisions and actions. If everyone shared a vivid view of the target customers and had visibility into customer feedback, then there would be less disagreement about what needs to be done for them."

Most leaders believe this and must remember this practice when expanding their strategy to multicultural markets. Review company mission and value statements and ensure that operations are organized to implement the business with a diverse set of needs in mind. Delivering an excellent customer experience requires a comprehensive view of the consumer. Consistent delivery of relevant services, products, benefits, and customer care should be a strong consideration when developing operational plans. Each area in the company with responsibility for implementing the relevant strategy must identify and close gaps to ensure a satisfied customer.

Testing Company Values

Customer centricity speaks to the heart of company values—a principal component of corporate culture. Companies must be willing to ask and honestly respond to the question of whether their implementation reflects their values with integrity. This is important because these carefully chosen words represent the beliefs and ideals that a company espouses and are the principles by which it operates. A company's values are its raison d'être

Values speak to a company's heart and intention to create genuine relationships with *all* its customers, so it's a critical starting point for any new market-expansion effort or for the recalibration of an existing effort to attract and retain multicultural sales. Integrity implies that the company's high-value customers, including those who are multicultural, can expect to have the same access to and experience with a company and its offerings.

It is often the case that company value statements were created many years ago. While there may have been a bit of editing over the years, they have stood the test of time. To be clear, the words are not the issue here. What is important is whether multicultural consumers feel like a company's value statements are reflected in the marketplace in a way that makes sense to them.

A large health-care client half-joked about the limited view some companies have about the applicability of company values to the customers they serve. He said, "Of course, leaders are committed to delivering a positive experience to all their customers as long as they look like them, speak English, and live in their neighborhoods."

Is he right? In many cases, he is, but I believe it's unintentional. As the country's demographics grow increasingly diverse, companies must do reality checks to determine whether their strategy implementation reflects the company's values truthfully and relevantly.

Put your company's mission and value statements to the test. Here are two sample mission statements

- Our innovative business model enables us to enhance access and deliver on a suite of assets that provides unmatched customer solutions.
- We bring innovative solutions to market, enabling us to serve our customers any way they want to be served.

The questions to ask when thinking about how well the mission statements apply to multicultural consumers might include the following:

- Is access enhanced for *all* people in the target market or just the people with whom decision makers are familiar? Do distribution channels and language options make the company's offerings fully accessible?
- Are solutions relevant to *all* high-value targets, including multicultural targets? Might all high-value targets consider your company's "unmatched customer solutions" to be the best solutions for them?
- Can service really be provided in a way that "any" consumer might need? Does the ability to serve high-value targets consider the possibility of a more diverse set of service requirements and wants? Does "any" consumer refer to a more familiar set of preferences?

Having integrity with mission and value statements requires an earnest examination of these types of questions and their implications.

Before any preliminary conversations with C-suite prospects, I always read the annual report, listen to the annual updates to shareholders on podcast, and read the 10-K report. By the time I step into their office, I'm clear about how the company positions itself and about its values—at least publicly.

I always ask for clarification on what the company means by its carefully selected words. Then I ask for examples of what these words look like in action. What does the implementation look like? What is the experience they're going for? What does it look like for persons of other cultural backgrounds and language abilities?

In most cases, the gaps become clear as they are talking, and they realize, in that moment, the company hasn't thought about the broader definition of their customers in the planning and execution of their strategy expansion to multicultural markets. For the most part, the oversights are unintentional, but it's important to note that intentional or not, the customer experience will either be positive or not so positive as a result. It is also apparent from these conversations that while many companies are engaging in multicultural marketing activity, there is little being done to ensure linkage between the experience being communicated and the experience being delivered.

Most of the time, high-value multicultural consumers and the characteristics and needs that set them apart aren't considered when implementing strategies. More importantly, the impact of these oversights isn't considered, which can make the difference between making the sale or handing it to the competition. At a time when most companies are trying to retain or regain consumer trust, the importance of demonstrating values with integrity is even greater. To achieve full alignment between company value statements and operations, it's important to develop an appreciation for the diverse nature of customers and their needs.

My mother and I are paying AARP members. We each receive a copy of the AARP magazine in English, which I can read but she cannot. AARP also has a wonderful expansive AARP website in English with valuable and interesting content. The Spanish-language site, however, is a condensed version that focuses on promoting their services and less on the valuable advice and information so prominently featured on the English site. The direct mail we receive at home is only in English. This lack of access to information and, ultimately, benefits among Spanish-dependent members results in two very different AARP member experiences. When I see articles I think she can benefit from, I must translate them into Spanish so she can derive the value from her membership benefits. This dynamic repeats in many Hispanic households, but it isn't in companies' best interest to depend on family members to deliver important company messages.

AARP's mission is "to enhance the quality of life for all as they age. The association advocates for positive social change and delivers value to members through information, advocacy, and service." Given the above example, AARP would be well served to examine whether they are really including "*all people* as they age" in this mission statement or just those who speak and read English. Understanding a company's existing and potential customer profiles makes a huge difference in the experience companies ultimately provide.

Consider that most budget-allocation or investment decisions for things like an updated technology platform, innovative new products, enhanced in-store experience, and line extensions for existing products (just to name a few) cannot possibly provide the highest ROI when they have been planned, designed, and implemented to be relevant to only 62 percent of the market (the other 38 percent being multicultural). And think about the fact that while nationally, the 62 percent number is accurate, in many regions or areas of the country, the concentration of multicultural populations is much higher. Businesses that don't implement relevantly are relying on less than two-thirds of the local population to fulfill 100 percent of their sales goals.

This type of investment will always be limited in its sales and customer satisfaction potential from the get-go, not to mention the ROI on the investment. Clearly, optimization radically expands the market potential.

Good Old-Fashioned Business Sense

Organizing for market-expansion success requires good old-fashioned business sense. There is no mystery about what is required to succeed in accelerating multicultural sales. It starts with the company's goals, its growth platforms, and its business strategy—irrespective of culture and ethnicity. Expanding into a new consumer market is about leveraging, not about changing a company's business goals and strategy; these never change.

There is no such thing as a multicultural strategy—or Hispanic, Asian, or African American strategy. There is only one business strategy to achieve growth. However, expanding this strategy to a new market—the multicultural market—does require delivering the company's strategy in a relevant manner. The key is relevant implementation, not a different strategy.

Successfully implementing the strategy requires adjustments to the respective implementation plans based on the company's cultural awareness and understanding of its high-value targets. The optimization of these implementation plans is what enables the company to act with integrity with its values, succeeding in making its offerings more relevant, more accessible, and more motivating to all targets—multicultural, generational, or otherwise.

Modeling and Organizing for Success

A large supermarket chain is a notable example of senior-level and company-wide commitment. This supermarket has been growing by double digits since it opened forty years ago. Sales growth is strong and improving quarter after quarter. Even so, management was aware that many of the trading areas where the chain had expanded wanted to expand their strategy to the Hispanic market.

Senior leadership assigned their best directors to assess the opportunity. They analyzed hundreds of their stores as well as competitive stores to understand the composition of their customer base and their cultural profiles. Management's goal was to define how to increase revenue among Hispanics by minimizing their need to shop elsewhere and without changing the company's business model. They did, however, assess how they would deliver their strategy in ways that would appeal to their Hispanics shoppers, including the product assortment, merchandising, and the store experience. They spent several weeks analyzing the implementation gaps they needed to close. They studied the competition, talked to Hispanic consumers in focus groups, and even followed them around the store while the customers shopped and answered questions about how they shop in the stores.

The goals were to learn about Hispanics' impressions of the current product assortment, how Hispanics felt when they shopped in their stores, and specific reasons why Hispanics shop and don't shop in their stores more frequently. Importantly, this research uncovered the reasons Hispanics also chose to shop in the competition.

The company also questioned their store personnel on their perceptions of Hispanic shoppers' shopping behavior and shopping experience. It was interesting to hear that the proportion of Hispanic to non-Hispanic shoppers in many stores was somewhat higher than the data had indicated. This meant that Hispanics represented a disproportionately higher share of the traffic in many stores and that perhaps Hispanics were traveling from outside the stores' trading areas to shop there.

However, management also discovered that Hispanics experienced communication challenges when shopping in the stores. This sometimes led to customers leaving the store without buying the items they were looking for because of the inability to communicate with employees and engage their help in finding the stocked items. In some cases, store managers voiced frustration that neither they nor their staff could speak Spanish, and the number of bilingual checkers was insufficient. Managers reported instances when they had to depend on bilingual customers to translate.

Because of their research, the company identified many opportunities. Management saw immediate opportunities for assigning bilingual employees to high–Hispanic-density stores. Management realized that important branding and value-proposition messages were lost on many Hispanic customers because the messages in English were not understood, so some stores were flagged for bilingual signage. They also made sure that branding and promotional signage in new markets included bilingual versions.

Management focused on developing a list of must-have authentic Hispanic products and brands, some of which are imports, and they worked on identifying Hispanic items they could provide under their store brand. Nielsen reported that after the 2008 recession, Hispanics had become more store-brand receptive than any other consumer group, so they identified and vetted several branding and packaging agencies and hired them to produce a new line of Hispanic items, which is now well over one hundred SKUs.

Marketing tested television and radio ads, the store's circular, and their social-media execution and identified several opportunities to improve messaging. To ensure appropriate alignment and relevance of messaging as well as language accuracy and media execution, they hired a Hispanic ad agency. The CEO, SVPs, VPs, and directors and all their buyers were involved in either the fact finding or the communication of discoveries and implementation changes.

This retailer continues to successfully expand its store presence and its Hispanic market growth. This example illustrates the type of commitment required to expand a strategy and the results companies can achieve when they optimize the delivery of their strategy.

For any strategy expansion effort to succeed, strategy and corporate culture must be aligned. While strategy and its implementation can be straightforward on paper, a corporate culture that believes in learning is what enables leadership to appreciate different consumer groups. Corporate culture is what drives a company's desire and its ability to understand a new culture in a way that can ensure relevant implementation. Importantly, cultural competency has the power to ensure that a company's values are reflected in its implementation with integrity, no matter the customers' ethnic or cultural background.

Chapter 7

Influences and Distractors

A company's capability to do well by its customers—diverse or otherwise—will depend in large part on the diverse makeup of its leadership and employees. By now, most companies understand or have at least heard about the value of having employees who are able to not only think about but also think like the diverse customers and employees they want to attract and retain. The benefits are better ideas, greater creativity, improved cultural fluency, and happier employees. However, for many companies, these benefits have not been perceived as sufficiently important to mobilize them to make the changes.

Let's be honest. As appealing as these benefits are, most leaders are not moved to shake up their organizations for the sake of creativity, different ideas, and happier employees. Few senior executives are willing to champion changes to attract and keep top diverse employees and to create work environments where diverse employees can be the best version of their "authentic selves." As fascinating as some of these benefits may be, if they are soft or qualitative and their impact on business performance is not self-evident, they are typically subject to question and scrutiny.

As a result, the business value of a diverse employee base at all levels of the organization is still not as compelling as we might think. One important reason leaders do not see the link between diversity and business performance is that they are typically insulated from the demographic change taking place in the country. Corporate headquarters are often in nondiverse geographies, their homes are in racially homogenous neighborhoods, and their friends all look like them. And they see the same homogeneity in the C-suite and the boardroom. The headquarters seldom sees the diversity on the front lines. They seldom see the value in having thinkers who can think, plan, and implement with the more diverse consumer reality that exists where they do business.

To some extent, it's easy to understand why it may be difficult for racially and culturally homogenous groups of leaders to support hiring, promoting, and working alongside colleagues who are racially and culturally different from them. As human beings, we all have unconscious biases based on our upbringing and past experiences that provide our lens for how we see the world and how we prioritize diversity within an organization irrespective of whether it makes sense for the business. Then there are leaders who outright refuse to acknowledge the demographic change taking place in the country and, in fact, believe that a company shouldn't have to change the makeup of its leadership and its employees nor change how it operates to appease a changing customer base; you'll recall this denier archetype from Chapter 3.

Whatever the reason, leaders have been slow to evolve the cultural makeup of their workforce; it is common knowledge that business performance is closely tied to how well companies align their products and services with consumers' constantly changing needs and wants, including greater diversity in the country's population. It's simply good business sense.

Part of ensuring a well-performing organization depends on a conscious effort by leadership to understand how the country's population has shifted and to ensure the needs of employees and customers are valued. Importantly, this must be modeled by top leadership. Moreover, to remain competitive, leaders must proactively work to position their companies for the *certain future* of constant change in demographics and consumer preferences. Avoiding change because of unfamiliarity and discomfort with people or situations that are different from the familiar only serves to perpetuate uncertainty, misperceptions, and fear within the organization.

Now more than ever, the goal should be to accelerate a level of comfort with and an appreciation for ethnic and cultural differences and to generate excitement about the benefits diverse employees and customers can contribute.

Business Case for Diversity

We could fill a book with the merits of shifting mind-sets and corporate cultures to invite an openness to cultural change, but in the end, leaders will always ask, "How is this going to help me with the investor community?" The business case for diversity must be proven. That's fine. Discuss the KPIs that matter and model the direct impact of increased diversity, cultural awareness, cultural competency, and cultural sensitivity on the company's enhanced capabilities and competitive positioning. In my experience, a straight line can be drawn from any of these capabilities to their impact on increasing sales, market share, and shareholder value.

The economic value of improved diversity in organizations has been studied and proven by the big five consultancies. For example, a 2015 McKinsey report entitled "Why Diversity Matters" indicates that "in the United States, there is a linear relationship between racial and ethnic diversity and better financial performance: for every 10 percent increase in racial diversity on the senior executive team, earnings before interest and taxes (EBIT) rise .08 percent." If the EBIT for a business segment is $1 billion, a .08 percent for every 10 percent increase in racial diversity translates into an $800,000 increase, which can be reinvested in the business by hiring more people, increasing marketing efforts, or making capital investments. Or it can be paid to shareholders, which will improve the value of the stock.

McKinsey also found that companies in the top quartile for racial and ethnic diversity are 35 percent more likely to have financial returns above their respective national industry medians. The report says, "Racial and ethnic diversity has a stronger impact on financial performance in the United States than gender diversity. Companies in the bottom quartile both for gender and for ethnicity and race are statistically less likely to achieve above-average financial returns than the average companies in the data set; that is, bottom-quartile companies are lagging rather than merely not leading. The unequal performance of companies in the same industry and the same country implies that diversity is a competitive differentiator shifting market share toward more diverse companies."

The implication that a more diverse organization is a competitive differentiator should immediately cause leaders to run (not walk!) to accelerate diversity efforts. However, to effectively mobilize an organization toward greater diversity, the specific financial advantages in quantifiable terms—EBITA, profits, and share value—should be clearly communicated. Simply put, how increased diversity and inclusion (D&I) will make or save the company money and how the company will improve its competitive position and shareholder value must be very clear. This financial clarity will help leaders make the mental shift from questioning and doubting the value of diversity efforts to championing it.

D&I should be clearly positioned as an enabler to meeting goals and desired business outcomes. For example, if a company's customer base includes (or has the potential to include) a substantial proportion of multicultural customers and the workforce lacks diversity, the company is handicapped, and sales among multicultural segments will not grow as quickly or at all compared to the competition.

In a recent conversation with Johanna Marolf, who led H&R Block's Latino effort for many years until 2016, she said, "When a company like H&R Block depends on sales success in our retail locations, of which many are in diverse neighborhoods, attracting a diverse workforce is fundamental. If a company doesn't have employees who reflect the customers who walk into its stores, it won't matter how great the products, pricing, or the marketing may be. A nondiverse sales organization simply can't be effective. So hiring the right people is important. However, equally important is the ability to retain the diverse employees being hired. Ensuring diverse employees receive the proper training, ensuring they see a career path, [and] ensuring they feel supported and valued becomes critical to not only being effective with customers but [also] how smoothly and profitably a company can operate."

Beyond making the business case, making those responsible for mobilizing the organization toward greater diversity and greater cultural competency accountable is critical. It should be tied to goals, raises, and bonuses. This raises the importance to another level.

Another way to get the company to see the linkage between diversity and profits is to involve key leaders in answering fundamental questions that will help move them from "why" to "how." If senior- and mid-level leaders are required to think through the company's goals, strategies, and results with the role and benefits of diversity in mind, the economic value will become self-evident, and they will become vested in the business case and necessary actions.

"The Why" — Making the Case

- What are the company's growth goals?
- What are the company's strategies and platforms for growth?
- What types of employees, consumers, customers, and vendors are important to the success of these strategies and platforms?
- What value can diverse employees, consumers, customers, and vendors have in the sustainable success of these strategies and platforms?
- What proportion of the top and bottom line do diverse segments have the potential to deliver?
- Does the company have the cultural awareness, competence, and credibility to successfully move toward its goals?

Once the "why"—in this case, the value—is clear, stakeholders will have the business reasons to make the necessary changes.

D&I Must Be Surgical

There is nothing more unproductive and damaging to company morale than the semblance of a D&I effort that isn't supported verbally or in practice by its leadership. The only way for a D&I strategy to gain traction and become sustainable is to assign its success to a senior-level non-Hispanic white male. I know this runs counter to the whole idea of having senior-level diverse leaders with cultural expertise to manage these initiatives, but this is a necessary first-stage strategy. This doesn't mean there shouldn't be a senior-level culturally diverse leader implementing the strategy. It means that someone even more senior assigned by the CEO is making sure the organization is complying with the implementation of the D&I strategy as a company mandate. This type of oversight is crucial for at least the first two to three years.

To start, D&I efforts should focus on the board, C-suite, and those business units that have been identified as growth platforms and where reflecting the mind-sets, needs, and wants of current and future diverse consumers is important, including functional areas that support them, such as market research, marketing, strategic planning and development, and implementation. For example, if a company's strategy depends on its ability to innovate, it must ensure its innovation team is diverse so innovation ideas have the best chance of meeting the needs of diverse customers.

If a company's growth platform depends on creating a frictionless customer journey across its technology and brick-and-mortar operations, it must ensure that store operations and divisional presidents are diverse, can identify diverse staffing needs, and can define what constitutes a frictionless customer-journey experience for its diverse high-value targets. If a company's point of differentiation is the breadth of its assortment, then it must ensure that leaders who plan category-growth strategies, buying, and merchandising are diverse and can provide insight into assortments that are relevant to high-value diverse targets. The appropriate research into customer needs and wants will enhance the innate knowledge among diverse leaders.

These are examples and are meant to illustrate that the importance for D&I is even more important to areas expected to deliver high value to all customers and drive growth for the company.

To start, define your diversity baseline by having HR conduct an employee census in the areas of greatest importance to the company's growth. In some cases, HR can work with leaders in key growth areas to determine if diverse employees can be moved from other areas in the company into areas where they can provide the greatest value.

I've worked with clients who have moved diverse employees into positions where they are more valuable and better suited and, in some cases, created efficiencies because these individuals can fulfill two roles. One of my life-insurance clients, for instance, staffed its customer-service-and-claims area with bilingual employees by moving them into these positions from other areas in the company. These employees could take both Spanish- and English-language customer calls; because of their additional cultural and language skills, they were given differential pay, making it a win-win-win for the company, its employees, and its customers.

In marketing, digital, and sales-management positions—areas where diversity was important to the company's growth goals—human resources worked to hire bilingual employees. This company also hired a sales manager to strengthen capabilities in regions where there were sales-agent gaps to call on diverse customers and prospects.

Many companies' products and services have become commodities. In such cases, companies find that customer experience along with innovation and technology are the areas on which they must differentiate themselves to succeed. Having relevant diverse employees in the right place (and at the right time) can give the company an important edge to innovate more relevantly and compete more effectively.

Closing diversity gaps in areas where there is personal and digital customer contact is especially critical. Think about how your multicultural customers engage with your call centers, claims department, sales associates, online chats, and online contact forms. If there is a gap in diverse leadership in these areas, service weaknesses go unnoticed, and dropped call rates and customer frustration increase. The right individual can quickly assess and determine how the current experience can be optimized so a company can retain the customers they attract more consistently.

When a company is in a solid "how" stage and planning or recalibrating its D&I strategy, key stakeholders should work together to determine important strategy components and considerations. A framework from my D&I work experience with several clients might be used if one doesn't already exist.

A Twelve-Step D&I Framework

1. Clearly communicate the business case for D&I.
2. Align D&I goals with the company's priorities.
3. Communicate the D&I business case and strategy to stakeholders. Use modules that speak to the various stages of D&I such as the following:

    • Revitalizing our business — business case and goals

- Empowering our talent — cultural awareness and competency training
- Expanding our awareness — filling the gaps and developing talent
- Internalizing the value — enabling growth

4. Assign a high-level change manager—preferably white and preferably male. (Interestingly, when a nondiverse senior leader is the executive sponsor and publicly champions diversity as a business imperative, there is no doubt as to the company's commitment to D&I.)

5. Require senior-management commitment and involvement in key areas. Successful CEOs dedicate quality time each month to discuss diversity processes and progress with their executives and consistently communicate its importance to the entire organization on a regular basis.

6. Push for the creation of a chief-diversity-officer position so D&I has a seat at the strategy table.

7. Align the organization's vision and core values in a way that supports the value of diversity and respect of cultural and gender differences.

8. Sensitize employees to cultural differences. Many successful companies implement cultural-sensitivity, unconscious-bias, and cultural-awareness training on a consistent basis, starting with the C-suite.

9. Monitor the organization's ability to develop diverse talent and match employees with leaders who do this well. Move employees away from leaders who do not.

10. Create diversity councils or roundtables where members of diverse cultures can share experiences and challenges and provide mutual support. Ensure a senior-level non-Hispanic white leader attends each one. The CEO attends at least quarterly.

11. Establish diversity-hire goals for the human-resources department and develop strategies for achieving them.

12. Create a monitoring tool that corresponds to each part of the organization and to overall goals. The CEO should present and

release progress publicly to validate the importance of the D&I change effort.

Monitoring D&I Success

Several years ago, I led a study of best practices in the grocery-retail industry for the Coca-Cola Retailing Research Council. As part of the process, I interviewed hundreds of executives at all levels of management grocery retail, CPG, and the trade organizations that represent these industries. I was able to compile a tool for monitoring D&I strategy implementation, which can serve as a great base on which your organization can build.

GOALS	MONITORING PROCESS
Improve Diverse Employee Retention	• Track diverse employee turnover along with and compared to overall employee-turnover rates. • Survey diverse employee satisfaction and attitudes about how the company treats them and how they feel about the company.
Increase Diverse New Hires	• Track diverse and white new hires in the field and at corporate, broken down by each ethnic group and gender. • Benchmark the company's diverse employee base against U.S. and local demographics. • Look at the proportion of diverse employee and management profiles to determine if they are proportionately reflective of the population.

Ensure That Diverse Employees Are Advancing through the Company	• Measure the percentage of diverse employees at various levels in the company two to three times a year to gauge improvement. Break it down by VPs, directors, district managers, corporate associates, store management, and department managers. • Track the percentage of diverse employees by ethnic group and gender that were promoted or moved laterally; lateral moves can be considered development.
Enhance the Company's Reputation in the Community	• Track relationships with and feedback from community leaders. • Track the number of referrals from community leaders. • Track press on company's progress or top position compared to others (or peer companies).
Report Progress to Senior Management	• Track communication with the CEO, the executive committee, and the diversity team to report on the number of initiatives started since last meeting, the number of meetings with executive committees and with district managers, the types of presentations given, and the type of support the organization is asking for. • Track frequency of progress meetings.

Modeling and Influencing from the Top

Alan Weiss, one of the most successful independent advisors to Fortune 500 companies in the country, believes that "the value of diversity and inclusion in any worthwhile transformation must be modeled by the

C-suite and the board of directors." When an organization needs to change behavior, attitudes, and culture, the most visible and respected leaders must head the change in a company's belief systems. According to Weiss, culture is simply a "set of shared beliefs and assumptions, often shaped over generations, that serve to direct company behavior.

To change culture, leaders must change belief systems by modeling different beliefs through their behavior." Sounds easy enough. So what's holding us back?

In large part, it's that the shared beliefs that drive culture and behavior in many companies come from a homogenous set of leaders. Today's corporate boards lack ethnic diversity and are overwhelmingly white, which is a direct result of the lack of diversity in the C-suite and Wall Street. Eighty-eight percent are non-Hispanic white, 7 percent are African American, 3 percent are Hispanic, and 2 percent are Asian.

In Jennifer Brown's book *Inclusion*, she paints a dismal picture of diversity in the C-suite. She indicates that "while 13.2 percent of the U.S. population is black, there are only five black CEOs. In 2015, Hispanics comprised 17 percent of the population, and only nine CEOs were Hispanics. And while 5.6 percent of the population is Asian, there are only ten Asian CEOs." The likelihood that these proportions will move organizations toward a more optimized diversity position in view of the 38 percent of nonwhite Americans is doubtful.

Some reasons for such small numbers of diverse CEOs is that companies and their executive search vendors do a poor job identifying diverse applicants and do a poor job developing diverse talent internally. In addition, diverse employees are often not included in or don't have access to the networking and bonding opportunities available to white employees and candidates.

The C-Suite is looked upon for leadership, for course setting, and for establishing the beliefs and values that its employees must espouse. But in matters of D&I, today's C-suite leadership is not leading relevantly. C-suite leaders must take bold steps to change their companies' beliefs and values and be willing to take significant steps toward modeling behavior that demonstrates both the emotional and cultural intelligence required to lead their organizations through a twenty-first–century marketplace—the most diverse in America's history.

This is no doubt difficult. After all, CEOs are only human. They were brought up and developed for their positions in another time. They developed their ideas for what it takes to successfully run a company from men who looked and thought alike. Their vision of the perfect workforce is based on an experience from the past.

Yet today's CEOs hold their positions because they are supposed to have the foresight to recognize and quickly respond to or even anticipate market forces—like demographic shifts—that require change. They're supposed to know when to regroup and work on the creation of an organization that includes diverse employees and management teams that make sense and help organizations succeed in the present and the future.

Further complicating matters is the fact that we are living in times of heightened hostility toward diverse populations. As mentioned in an earlier chapter, the time since the 2016 election has been extremely disruptive to companies and multicultural consumers alike. Hispanics, Asians, and many other ethnicities are living in threatening and uncertain times. Misunderstood "nationalism" is at an all-time high. Our government is unfriendly toward immigrants and their children. Immigrants are associated with security concerns. Deportation threats receive daily news coverage. This hostile climate impacts not only undocumented populations but also their U.S.-born families. The idea of building the wall and protecting our borders is fueling growing discord among communities. Immigration reform has become an increasingly contentious topic, and the threat of the DACA repeal affects over seven hundred thousand Dreamers.

Although company CEOs report being stunned and unsure where this will end, some CEOs see through the rhetoric and have taken steps to distance themselves from the current administration's councils and from ideology and actions that run counter to their values. Importantly, CEOs are clearly speaking to the business case for ensuring their companies benefit from the value diverse employees can contribute to their businesses. However, these same beliefs are not translating into bold steps to increase diversity in the boardrooms, the C-suite, and top leadership positions. The beliefs that ostensibly guided these leaders to speak up boldly in favor of their immigrant employees appear to be at odds with the beliefs that limit diversity at senior levels of their organizations.

This said, many companies have been training and mobilizing their organizations toward greater D&I mastery. There are notable examples of organizations that have created and embedded the best D&I practices into their way of doing business.

Diversity Inc. selects the Top 50 Companies for Diversity on a yearly basis, and in 2017, they included such industry giants as AT&T, which leverages a dozen or so employee resource groups (ERGs) and employee networks (ENs) where employees interested in distinct cultures can expand their knowledge about people who are different from them. ERGs also provide opportunities to find models and mentors among participating leadership who model the desired behavior. ERG and EN memberships topped 134,000. And ERG volunteer hours reached a record of 369,910 hours. Ernst & Young holds its leaders accountable for equitably mentoring, sponsoring, and advancing talent and empowers its people to have courageous conversations about pressing D&I issues.

Feedback mechanisms and accountability are common practices at Ernst & Young and Johnson & Johnson, where managers have clear D&I goals on which they are assessed during performance reviews. Managers who consistently meet goals and demonstrate an acumen around inclusive leadership are rewarded with fast advancement within the company. These companies make it clear that their performance is critical not only for the day-to-day health of the business but also for the advancement and success in their careers.

Whether it's about incorporating messages of inclusion throughout the business, leveraging an employee for his or her specific expertise and knowledge about certain customers, or ensuring examples of D&I are visible within leadership ranks, these actions demonstrate commitment to a diverse employee and customer base that inevitably translates into enhanced business performance.

Chapter 8

Frameworks for Success

Applying Horizon Two thinking from the Three Horizons Framework discussed in Chapter 5 requires rethinking how some companies have been pursuing multicultural market sales. In the *Alchemy of Growth*, Baghai, Coley, and White suggest that companies should be spending 20 percent of their time and resources on Horizon Two activities to expand their strategy to new consumer markets that have the potential to contribute a significant and growing part of the company's future revenue.

This requires that companies recognize the potential to use their current strengths and assets to pursue a large and growing consumer opportunity that represents the potential to generate substantial profits in the one- and three-year horizons. Achieving this full economic potential requires gaining a position of competitive advantage, typically achieved by expanding and implementing a company's strategy into a new market in a relevant manner.

The Profit-Lens Guidelines

Organizing to gain a position of advantage in a new consumer market like the multicultural market is a crucial and recognized path to continued growth and value building. In fact, the market rewards competitive advantages in new markets with higher PE ratios based on expected future performance.

Corporate leaders must learn to look at this growth opportunity through a different lens, and they must be very clear and focused on what, why, and how they will deliver on their current strategy to multicultural consumers so they can maximize revenue and market-share growth in the short term and profit growth in the midterm. Here's a ten-point profit-lens checklist to assist in gaining clarity on what needs to be considered and employed.

1. Strategic Clarity

Remain true to your company's business goals and strategic focus. The goal in expanding a company's business strategy to a new consumer market is to benefit from a new revenue stream. The premise is that a company's current strategy, its capabilities, and its assets have already proven successful at meeting revenue goals and can be leveraged further to enter a new market in much the same manner as is currently being used to target other consumer markets. The U.S. multicultural consumer market represents enormous growth potential, and the future of growth will, in part, depend on gaining a competitive advantage in your industry among this new target population. This will require adapting implementation tactics, not strategy.

2. C-Suite Clarity

It's critical for the CEO to be involved in and guide the management of strategy-expansion efforts—it could be said, even more critical than for Horizon One core implementation—because the CEO is the most likely to see the midterm revenue-growth opportunity the multicultural consumer market represents despite not producing ROI in the short term. The CEO will understand the need for budget flexibility to keep the expansion on track.

3. Organizational Clarity

Organizing to expand a company's strategy to multicultural consumer markets is best achieved by assigning senior-level leaders with an entrepreneurial management style who are skilled at business building. Leaders whose management styles emphasize core business strategies focused on protecting existing markets and value rather than building them are seldom a good fit for this role and should be avoided if possible.

4. Value Clarity

Do the homework to clearly identify high-value multicultural consumer targets and define the value of their contribution to revenue and market-share growth now and in the next three years. Then get to know them—intimately—so implementation of the strategy can be as relevant as possible. The goal should be to gain or maintain a position of competitive advantage where this consumer is concerned.

5. Target Clarity

Focus on segments of the multicultural consumer market that align with the same needs, tastes, and wants as the company's core targets. Focus and invest in increasing the penetration of your existing brands among multicultural category users. Don't invest in developing the category.

6. Decision Clarity

Once you understand the revenue potential, develop the implementation plan, allocate a flexible budget commensurate with the task, assign senior leaders fit to building the brand in a new consumer market, and then implement with conviction. Planning and implementing "one-off initiatives or projects" is incongruous with expanding a strategy into a new consumer market and has no place here. Terminology such as *initiative* and *project* imply it has a beginning and an end. Expansion effort work has no end; to drive future growth, it needs to be long-term and sustainable.

7. Integration Clarity

Expanding a strategy into a new consumer market requires the entire organization. Expanding a strategy into a new market is not a marketing project. The same areas in the company that implement the strategy in core-consumer markets are required, along with a culturally competent senior leader to ensure all areas make relevant implementation adjustments.

8. Optimization Clarity

Define the necessary optimization across required areas in the organization to ensure a customer journey that is as seamless as it is for everyone else and ensure they are reached and communicated to effectively.

9. Metrics Clarity

While the business goals and strategies for Horizon Two–level expansions are the same as for the core business, they require focus on different metrics that are more appropriate to new ventures. Strategy-expansion activity success should be evaluated based on revenue and market-share increases, NPV, and set milestones. Metrics used to evaluate established core businesses such as profit, return on invested capital, and cash flow should be avoided. These metrics are not relevant until the strategy is well established—one to three years out on average.

10. Accountability Clarity

The framework must be clear. The goals must be clear. The market must be clear. The implementation must be clear. And the rewards or consequences for performance must be clear. Expanding a company's strategy to a new market is especially valuable when the target market is experiencing aggressive growth and represents significant future potential for companies, allowing them to achieve a position of advantage among their competitive set if they implement relevantly. As such, focusing on multicultural targets to grow sales are a means to this end, not the end itself. The goal is to grow revenue and market share among a new set of consumers by using a company's proven strategy and capabilities.

Optimization versus Change

Optimize is defined as making "the best or most effective use of a situation, opportunity, or resource." If we were speaking of optimizing a microscope's viewing performance, we might adjust the lens or create a better lens; we wouldn't change the way the microscope works or what it is intended to do. Optimizing the implementation of a strategy is not about changing "what" the company does, what it stands for, or its business model. Optimizing is about adjusting, not entirely changing, "how" the company executes to increase relevance and effectiveness among new targets.

Importantly, optimizing how a company expands its strategy to multicultural markets in an integrated manner from planning, implementation, and measurement is critical to success. It's important for those leading the expansion implementation to understand that optimizing processes, functions, and operations is required to increase relevance among the new targets. Relevant optimization of implementation tactics will also reflect a genuine alignment between the company's actions and its values.

Successful optimization requires an organization to have or develop cultural competency. Market research, insights analysis, and discussion about high-, medium-, and low-priority buying considerations can help define critical success factors for optimization. The focus should be placed on areas that will have the greatest impact on sales. For instance, enhancements that allow a multicultural consumer to easily access and benefit from a brand's consumer promise should be prioritized. The promise doesn't change; how the company delivers the promise is optimized to ensure multicultural targets can benefit just like the company's core customers.

The speed and degree to which the optimization is undertaken for certain areas will, at times, depend on several factors, including other internal optimization work taking place, such as upgrading and consolidating outdated legacy-infrastructure systems, remodeling stores, or acquiring a new website platform. However, make sure that large-scale updating, replacement, and reprogramming efforts are optimized for the new market along with everyone else during the planning stage. This will ensure that new assets are optimized with consumer and company needs in mind from the outset. It is expensive and time consuming to realize that wonderful new capabilities have limited relevance to some consumers, especially after making significant investments.

Other considerations that tend to limit the speed with which optimization work is undertaken for certain areas include interdependencies between two or among three areas where one area is working on a large-scale overhaul project and another area depends on the completion of the work to proceed with their optimization. Optimization speed may also depend on the capabilities of a third-party vendor. For instance, the finance industry is currently working on robotic technology to support financial advisors, and one company is designing the technology that will enable advisors to operate in different languages; this is optimization foresight.

It's important for key decision makers in the organization to be aware of and accountable for collaborating during the optimization process. This will create greater consideration toward interdependencies among functions and will engender greater internal accountability. When areas responsible for carrying out an improvement, a change, or a purchase are aware that carrying out a certain part of the work is dependent on another area's delivery or completion of their task, it is likely those responsible will take the tasks more seriously.

Implementation optimization work needs a budget that is commensurate to the task. Until now, multicultural activity has not been managed as a market-expansion effort. Companies haven't managed or budgeted for them as the revenue-growing efforts they represent. Marketing managers are often forced to either use their marketing budget or beg key areas of the organization to make optimization adjustments with their budgets. This is often met with resistance and refusals. Optimizing implementation tactics across the organization has actual associated costs. However, investment in optimization work implies low risks because the current strategy and implementation are proven and have already produced positive results.

D&I Is Not the End-All Solution

Many companies believe that having a D&I strategy is the solution to help a company expand its strategies to a new segment. There are many flaws in this type of thinking. D&I on its own is not set up to grow sales among diverse consumers any more than it can grow sales among any of a company's existing consumer targets.

In most organizations, D&I is within the purview of human resources and is key to the creation of the organization's vision to increase diversity, to ensure inclusion, and to create a work climate that leverages diversity to improve company performance. While increasing the company's level of diversity has the potential to produce solutions with greater relevance and that align to the needs and wants of diverse targets, it takes more than culturally competent thinking to complete a value chain.

On one occasion, I was preparing for a presentation with a client from a large retail pharmacy organization who said, "Our communications director believes we ought to start the presentation by saying that Hispanics are important to the company because we have a strong culture of diversity and inclusion." My polite response was that the company hadn't decided to target Hispanics because it has a culture of D&I any more than it targets women or seniors for the same reason. I added that the reason this company or any company decides to target Hispanics, women, seniors, or Hispanic women and seniors is because they represent a strong opportunity for increased revenue. There was dead silence on the line. Long story short, the client recognized the wisdom of the reasoning, and we did not start the presentation as suggested by the communications director.

D&I has a specific role in helping companies increase their market relevance, but be careful not to assume that just because D&I is usually made up of a group of diverse individuals or because resource groups exist where ideas for multicultural markets are tested, it is the solution for successfully expanding a company's business strategy to another segment. New multicultural or diverse consumer targets must be approached as part of the larger business context.

The same methodical approach used by a company to expand its strategy to any new market must be applied to multicultural targets, and responsibility for the expansion must be owned and managed by the respective heads of business units or divisions—decision makers with P&L responsibility.

It Takes More Than Marketing

When marketers think about targeting and engaging multicultural consumers to grow sales for the company, marketing is single-mindedly where most companies focus, but this is a mistake. I often overhear marketers at conferences tout their Hispanic-market tactics. I hear about Spanish-language brochures or pamphlets, the new Hispanic marketing manager, the cool community events or sponsorships, and the company's decision to adopt a culture of D&I to improve its multicultural efforts.

While these efforts can be strong tactical steps, none either individually or collectively stand a chance of producing substantive revenue results. Think about it. When was the last time your company decided to expand its activities to a new market to benefit from a new revenue stream and relied exclusively on marketing tactics? It doesn't make sense. And that is my point: common sense tells you there is much more to expanding into a new market than investing in a few marketing tactics.

Growing multicultural sales effectively requires a comprehensive and holistic company-wide effort. Marketing is one of the last steps to take once the company is set up to deliver on the strategy—and not a minute sooner. You want to be able to keep and hopefully delight the customers your marketing attracts; otherwise, your marketing investment will be largely wasted.

Responsible and Accountable

Successfully expanding a company's strategy to another market segment requires a leadership team with an entrepreneurial spirit as well as implementation support assigned to key areas in the company. Assembling the necessary management team includes those responsible for the company's value chain. These decision makers have the responsibility and are accountable for understanding the new consumer market being targeted and the revenue growth opportunity it represents. They must also understand the critical success factors for delivering on the company's strategy relevantly and the required optimization work.

Successful strategy expansion into any market domestically or globally requires all hands on deck. In any given month when I'm discussing multicultural efforts either at a conference or at a client site, I hear executives say, "I know we do some of that [target Hispanics], but I'm not sure who does it" or "Somebody in the company is working on that [Hispanic], but it's not us." Responses like this signal a disconnect from what should be a well-known and widely supported effort to generate revenue in a new market. It indicates internal misalignment.

Effectively growing sales among a new target market takes a village, as they say. Organizing to serve a new target (or several) requires cross-functional and cross–business-line participation and support. Leaders must be informed and engaged to support efforts that will successfully expand the company's strategy. Rewards for performance and consequences or lack thereof should be clear.

Integration

If important revenue-growth activity in a new consumer market is not integrated into the larger strategy-delivery effort, it will suffer a quick death. It's that simple. Some will putter along through false starts and stops, while others will simply be dead on arrival. The causes and symptoms of this are covered extensively in Chapters 3 and 4. Marketers and their agency partners have been through a series of models and concepts meant to generate revenue from new multicultural targets, but these have been only marginally successful.

You can repeat the missteps, or you can learn from past experiences or the experience of others. Then you can hit the reset button, reframe the work as a strategy expansion to a new market, and put your best foot forward. One way to put your best foot forward is by ensuring the strategy implementation is integrated into the overall delivery of the company's strategy. However, putting your best foot forward requires leadership that is convinced the effort will grow the company's revenue stream. It requires leadership that is committed to expanding the company's existing business model to the U.S. multicultural market.

I define *integration* as the inclusion of the new market—multicultural consumers—into the company's strategy planning and implementation process. The alternative is to retrofit as an afterthought, as many companies have done in the past, with poor results and lots of frustrated individuals. Any good leader knows that the delivery of a strategy is just as important as the strategy itself. This is an area where many companies falter in pursuit of new markets, not just multicultural. Effectively delivering on a strategy requires close coordination and communication between those who plan and those who execute the strategy. This is important because those who plan the strategies are often big-picture and long-term thinkers. They focus on the destination and outcomes, while those who implement the strategy are often short-term thinkers who focus on process and actions.

Integration means that those responsible for strategy and those responsible for implementation must communicate closely so the planning process and the actions taken are consistent. Those responsible for implementation must understand the business performance at stake so they understand the importance of the integration. Detail-oriented implementers familiar with execution realities will raise questions, talk about risks, and bring up roadblocks. Those who own the expansion and delivery of the strategy to multicultural markets will need to help them understand by offering a road map that answers questions and helps them improve their understanding of the new market—especially around economic value and cultural competence. Implementers must be able to see how risks can be mitigated and embrace the need for integration and optimization.

Integration is something most companies do innately but struggle to do when it involves a new and unfamiliar target segment. However, the sooner the company can make this mental transition, the sooner it can successfully expand its strategy to accelerate sales among its new multicultural targets. Adopting this focus and conversation will create cohesiveness and collaboration and will advance the company's pursuit of revenue growth.

Modeling Integration and Optimization

In the case of a large auto aftermarket retailer, the SVP of marketing and the SVP of merchandising realized that despite the Hispanic-market success already enjoyed by the company, there was tremendous opportunity for accelerating revenue even further. The key question the executive committee asked was this: How much additional revenue potential exists in the Hispanic market? They committed to a complete assessment of their organization on both the B2C and B2B parts of their business. They realized the opportunity extended to its ability to support the needs of its commercial customers with a large Hispanic clientele.

A representative leadership team was assembled from all areas in the company, including store development, finance, sales analytics, marketing, merchandising, operations, human resources, training and development, infrastructure, and digital (including those responsible for in-store digital screens, the website, and the customer-service 800 number). The analytics team segmented several thousand stores across a variety of variables and performed regression analysis, which identified business-driver variables across their store base. The model identified highest-opportunity stores and stores where the opportunity wasn't great currently but where growth acceleration potential existed. The model also generated incremental sales-volume potential by store based on a regression analysis.

Next, they assessed how high-opportunity stores were aligned to the needs of Hispanic customers. This included an assessment of bilingual branding and promotional signage quality and requirements. A process was developed to communicate merchandising needs to marketing and to track the approval and delivery of the right products. Creative and media plans were assessed and adjustments made to network and local buys to ensure coverage in markets where the highest-opportunity stores were located. The creative was also optimized to be consistent in tone with the brand's image.

Human resources analyzed its bilingual-employee availability and location, and they worked on plans with local district managers to create "staff to coverage" schedules and a regular reporting process from district managers who oversaw high-opportunity stores. This analysis included whether bilingual field-management staff existed in required geographies. A short language-screening test consisting of a set of structured questions was developed to assess Spanish fluency among future Hispanic hires. Because the recruiting portal generated few bilingual candidates, recruitment methods were expanded to include in-store applications and interviews. Training and development materials were assessed and sent to third-party partners for optimization. Cultural-sensitivity training was considered for store managers and district managers.

In-store digital screens were optimized to include bilingual information on the top ten car makes and models owned by high-value Hispanic targets. In-store staff was trained to provide this information bilingually based on a quick assessment of the customer's preference. The 800-number greeting was rerecorded with a professional voice with a native speaker's accent, and the system was optimized so Spanish-speaking callers did not fall out of the Spanish language tree of VRU.

Merchandising analyzed the best-selling items in high-opportunity stores and developed a plan to expand distribution of relevant assortments to high-opportunity stores. Company management visited stores that sell car accessories, including making visits to competitors. The team quickly identified several items, including culturally relevant graphics, decals, flags, sports-team logo merchandise, license-plate frames, and snacks and beverages to add to their store assortment in high-opportunity stores. Many B2B customers were visited in several markets to identify relevant support that could be provided, including specific products and bilingual collateral.

In addition, because rapport and sales performance are closely linked, an assessment of whether Hispanic-owned shops were handled by bilingual sales managers was conducted in high-opportunity markets. This assessment, which lasted several months, and its recommendations and budgeting process were followed closely by the executive committee, including the CEO. Upon completion, a timeline was developed for integrating the recommendations into the company's operational plans with short- and midterm implementation schedules along with milestone reporting periods.

Organizing for success requires top-to-bottom clarity on what a company wants to achieve and why, what it needs to do to succeed, and how it will hold those responsible accountable for performance. Decision makers must be clear on the differences between optimization of implementation tactics and changing the way the company does business, and they must be clear that expansion implies the first, not the latter.

Decision makers must know better than to relegate important revenue-growth initiatives to human resources or to think that marketing will be the end-all solution to a successful expansion. Approaching an expansion in this manner will not succeed. Like any expansion undertaking, efforts to grow revenue in a new consumer market must be integrated into the way the company does business, even as it requires adaptation to make implementation tactics relevant to the new market.

Decision makers must realize that expansion efforts require commensurate investments. These investments can be incremental, or they can be reallocated from another venture. Knowing the new market's future revenue-growth potential should always be the rationale for moving forward and making budget allocation decisions to get the job done correctly.

Strategy-expansion decisions are always preceded by solid assessment, opportunity sizing, projections, and a lot of foresight. Once the decision is made, it behooves decision makers to organize and do the job right and stick to the plan. No strategy bears fruit overnight. As with other growth initiatives, domestic or global, new markets require investment of time and money. It's vital to be patient and stay the course.

Chapter 9

Organizational Readiness

Organizational readiness to implement a strategy is fundamental to success—irrespective of the target market. Success in any initiative requires an intimate familiarity with the company's goals and strategies and the target market. Taking it a step further, it requires an understanding of how consumer targets are likely to engage with the company—whether it is in person, digitally, or by telephone—and what must be in place to ensure customers have a positive experience and make a purchase, return to make subsequent purchases, and tell others to buy from a company.

Multicultural targets can include consumers of different ethnic backgrounds, nationalities, cultures, and language preferences, but they have one thing in common with the rest of your targets: they are category users, which is why they've been identified as high-value targets for expanding your existing strategy. Here is where it gets tricky. Because they may have different reference points for how they view the category and how they view a brand, the way they prefer to engage and buy may differ from other consumers in your target. Therefore, the organization must be ready to serve them by becoming relevant to their preferences. At a minimum, this means in the areas that touch them and in areas where the competition is serving them seamlessly. These areas could include the experience they will encounter in your stores, online, on the phone, and through the mail.

Because the experiences customers have through a company's touch points are critical to retention and positive word of mouth, it's important to include the back-end operations that support how a company appears and engages on the front end. Typically, when a company can clearly sequence the right support to the touch points along the customer's purchase funnel, it can readily identify the quick fixes as well as short- and midterm optimization opportunities. Operational, infrastructure, and organizational areas that require relevant optimization will vary by industry and business model. The following optimization examples provide some guidance, but each company must decide which areas are the most crucial in the delivery of its strategy.

Organizational Structure

Organizing to implement relevantly is critical to successfully expanding a strategy to new consumer-market segments. The CEO must be vocal about the benefits derived from any organizational structure change, highlighting the company's strategy and the decision to expand the strategy to a new market because of strong forecasts of revenue potential. One or two senior executives should be assigned by the CEO (with ongoing accountability to the CEO) for ensuring company-wide commitment and accountability.

Dissolving multicultural groups is the next priority to achieve full integration. Those who have been working on multicultural efforts up to now as a separate group should be allocated to business units and areas within them that make most sense depending on each person's experience and expertise. These could be brand management, marketing, marketing research, sales, human resources, store operations, digital, and so on. Depending on the organization, there might be dual reporting lines to the senior executive stewards leading the strategy expansion and the department heads to which individuals are reassigned.

Some may consider this reorganization approach drastic. But it is not. As discussed in previous chapters, expanding a company's existing strategy and business model to a new market is a business strategy that requires CEO and senior-level involvement, and it requires the "A-Team" to manage the relevant delivery of the strategy.

To be clear, we are talking about a Horizon Two endeavor meant to capture the business potential of a new revenue stream, and we are talking about building value for the company into the future. We are not talking about a fleeting marketing initiative for a brand with an established core-consumer base.

Marketing Research

Market research is a critical function in any expansion plan and is vital to providing deep insights to those leading the effort and those responsible for relevant delivery of the strategy. It will be important to shift how the marketing-research team views the scope of the research they manage. Because marketing to multicultural consumers has been viewed as a separate endeavor, research departments are not accustomed to including multicultural targets when they plan and design studies or when buying syndicated data.

To do this effectively, researchers will need to become familiar with a new consumer target and a broader set of providers with multicultural market expertise. They will need to partner with and learn about the research methodologies that are most appropriate. They will also need to educate their new partners on the company's practices and study types and timing that are commonly deployed by the company. Market researchers will also need to become familiar with myriad syndicated data providers that include multicultural consumers in their studies and subscribe to those studies that will enhance their knowledge about category and brand results for their industry and brands.

Data Analytics

Data analytics has become a critical foundation for providing business direction. Companies must think about the types of reporting that will be important to obtain the results of the strategy-expansion and implementation work. Identifying and acquiring the respective internal and external data sources to monitor and analyze multicultural behavior across sales, marketing, loyalty programs, website traffic, and any area that the company typically analyzes to optimize the sales, efficiency, and effectiveness of its efforts will be critical.

Defining approaches to identify which existing and past customers are multicultural may be useful. Although not perfect, developing or acquiring a strong surname list to help identify those multicultural consumers that are already customers and developing an algorithm is always a good start. These names could be coded so the system recognizes them, and a proprietary data base can be developed.

Any organization that values real-time performance data for all its products and consumer segments must ensure its infrastructure platforms are set up to generate these reports on demand. IT teams should work to identify and program the necessary fields that will be useful to track established KPIs where they do business.

This data can be used in several ways, including by retail-development teams that can match sales variables with multicultural-consumer segment penetration within the footprint of their stores. The company can then cluster stores based on multicultural variables and criteria important to the company's reporting needs. This view of the data provides important sales and demographic information by store clusters, which can inform decisions on hiring a more diverse staff, defining where bilingual signage is most productive, adapting merchandising to sales activity, and enhancing product assortment based on purchase trends. Companies must think through the type of reporting they require to monitor multicultural results and optimize their infrastructure platforms to generate the data reports they require.

Information Technology (IT) and the Customer Experience

Information technology (IT) infrastructure in today's technologically advanced business environment is a crucial management tool used to deliver products and customer support, communicate with customers, and provide the data needed to improve customer experiences. While the actions of IT are driven by decision makers within the organization, IT is a foundation to many company touch points and profoundly impacts the customer experience with most companies. Companies that rely on letters, statements, and notices to communicate with customers require their IT systems to generate dual-language communication.

Banks, insurance companies, and wireless-telephone companies mail thousands of offers with applications, thank-you letters, past-due payment letters, renewal forms, brochures for new product offerings, user guides, warranties, rebate forms, and billing or bank statements—all of which are critical to the business. It's important for them to avoid having their mail immediately tossed because of a language barrier. When there's a language barrier, it doesn't matter how urgent or important the requested actions may be; those actions simply won't be understood or acted upon by a sizable proportion of customers or would-be customers. Important communication is only effective when it is understood.

The optimization work often involves coding customer records as well as new programming tailored to customer and company needs. IT must define what needs to be optimized to support relevant communication through sales channels and customer service. The system should be programmed to direct each piece of communication based on the language preferences of the recipient.

Many companies are challenged by outdated legacy systems and data stored on different platforms, but it is important to address the most fundamental platforms. This is challenging and time consuming at first, but once it's done, the work is mostly focused on updating. IT platforms should be able to target specific offers to customers who meet specific profile or behavior characteristics, regardless of cultural or ethnic background. The goal should be to facilitate access to the company's offerings so it's convenient and easy regardless of the touch point where the customer chooses to access the product or service.

Many companies rely on infrastructure to enhance customers' shopping experience and facilitate sales and other transactions through kiosks, self-checkout, and payment screens. During an infrastructure assessment for a wireless company, we visited dozens of stores all over the country where we observed customers of all cultures and language abilities interacting with the various digital assets in the stores, including the check-in screen where customers signed in to be serviced, the payment kiosks, the digital showroom that presents the latest phones and features, and the TV screens playing commercials. The difference in the level of engagement between younger generations (under age thirty-five) who spoke English and older generations (over age thirty-five) who weren't as fluent in English was striking and represented a missed opportunity. One of the first things we addressed was reprogramming these assets so they were bilingual. We also updated the images of people on the phone and tablet displays to better reflect the diversity of the customer base.

This scenario repeats itself across a multitude of industries. Companies spend millions to provide a positive in-store experience, but when infrastructure is not optimized, a significant group of multicultural customers are left out, and companies miss the opportunity to engage the customer with the product or service—and likely lose the sale to the competition. It's important to consider that when companies make investments in infrastructure that is not optimized to its full potential for *all* customers, it will not generate the intended return on investment because it will be only partially effective.

Companies also rely on infrastructure to limit costs by automating activities that would otherwise be handled by employees. It's important to assess whether the company's infrastructure supports the quick and comfortable transition and adoption of automation among multicultural targets. This is the only way to ensure that these customers quickly grow less dependent on people and more dependent on technology to shop for their products. Cost-saving opportunities include developing the mechanisms and communications to help customers transition from tech support delivered via a live person on the phone to tech support by email or chat and to use kiosks to make payments instead of teller windows or customer-service desks.

When a language barrier exists between a customer and kiosk because the screens aren't understood, the kiosk becomes just another piece of store decor as far as some multicultural targets are concerned. The phone will keep ringing for live support (which will hopefully offer bilingual support lest the company miss out on a sales- or customer-satisfaction opportunity altogether). Underoptimized infrastructure investments exist across all types of businesses, while the demand for more expensive live support remains or grows.

Define the ways your company relies on infrastructure to provide great service and access to your products and services, to communicate with your targets effectively, to cut costs, to provide critical reporting, and to identify the type of optimization required to successfully expand your company's strategy to target multicultural consumers.

Relevant Products and Services

Expanding a company's strategy to a new market like multicultural targets doesn't mean new products must be developed or procured. As discussed in Chapter 8, the goal of expanding a company's strategy to a new market segment is to grow penetration of the company's existing brands and products among high-value multicultural category users. Most companies already sell the products and services their multicultural targets want.

There are exceptions. For instance, some multinational companies like Nestlé and Procter & Gamble have hugely successful brands in Latin America and in Asia. Recognizing the large Latin American and Asian population in the United States, these companies complement their U.S. assortments with brands from Mexico and Asia. This is a notable example of optimizing assortment to increase relevance, gaining a competitive advantage, and delivering differentiation value to the retail customers that decide to carry the items.

Ordinarily, however, strategy expansion does not involve finding "white space" in the new market. "White space" activities are typically long-term Horizon Three activities. They are risky and expensive, and their break-even time frames are long. Avoid R&D and new product-development work to attract the new multicultural market unless there is demand for the same types of products among the broader core target. For example, multicultural consumers are driving many product and service trends that non-Hispanic white customer segments are increasingly enjoying. However, pursuing product development with ethnic flavors is a different strategy—one that focuses on capitalizing on niche market trends to cater to changing mainstream consumer-taste preferences. Trying to expand this strategy to multicultural consumers likely would not work. Organizations that pursue these types of strategies are focused on product leadership and are willing to take bold steps.

A large retail organization was so interested in optimizing its product assortment and merchandising that it conducted a thorough analysis of the types of items Hispanic "do it yourselfers" purchase most across more than five thousand stores nationwide. The assessment included an analysis of the most frequent auto part sales based on analysis of the top ten cars (and model years) Hispanics own in all their footprints so specific stores could be well stocked with those parts. This didn't mean the retailer was changing its core merchandise mix; it meant it was willing to optimize its mix in specific stores according to the cars Hispanics drive. The effort included compiling a list of snacks and beverages Hispanics typically impulse-buy and identifying unique novelty items with Hispanic motifs and designs on floor mats, car-seat covers, license-plate frames, and flags as well as religious items purchased by Hispanics for protection. The company's merchandisers then found providers for these items and added them to the assortment in the right stores.

Optimizing assortments to increase relevancy among Hispanics to accelerate sales growth will work for many retailers.

Employees Mirroring Customers

The truism that employees are our greatest assets is more relevant than ever when delivering on a strategy that depends on understanding, communicating, and connecting effectively with multicultural targets. These targets may have distinct cultural buying references and influencers and may feel more connected to the sales representative if they are able to communicate in their language of choice—even when they speak English. Employees mirroring customers in key areas of the organization, including management, optimizes this customer-service capability.

As discussed in Chapter 7, companies are increasingly attuned to employee diversity. They know it fuels creativity and positions the company to be more responsive and adaptive to the communities it serves. Assessing how HR's hiring and retention processes can be optimized is a crucial step. Oftentimes recruiters don't have the capability to refer diverse candidates to their clients for executive positions. Online application processes can also be a barrier to prospective employees; they often don't feel user-friendly to multicultural job seekers. It's also important to make in-language applications available and to ensure that the transactions take into account cultural insights and sensitivities.

A large retailer relied solely on online applications and tests to source and qualify job applicants. Upon closer examination, it realized that very few multicultural job applicants apply online despite posters in the stores announcing they were hiring. Meanwhile, store managers were desperate for Spanish speakers. The retailer realized it had to allow individual stores to accept hard-copy applications and administer tests and conduct interviews in the store. Accommodations such as these are sometimes necessary, and companies must be flexible.

The benefits of mirroring consumers in customer-facing positions are obvious positions, but functional areas at corporate, those in call centers (or chat), and social-media management also require multilingual employees. In some cases, a company is not able to immediately add headcount, but when HR and area management identify language needs, HR can identify employees who have those language skills internally and place them in an area of the company where their cultural and linguistic strengths are leveraged and their skills recognized through differential pay.

In another case, a well-established life-insurance company discovered it would be important to their sales efforts to hire a Hispanic sales manager who subsequently hired and trained dozens of bilingual independent agents. Additionally, they identified language-skills needs in customer service, claims, marketing, creative, and digital. They were able to successfully identify and move bilingual employees to customer-facing positions at headquarters, where they were more valuable. In some cases, the job responsibilities for the employees were expanded such that they could support their respective areas in dual language. HR prepared to fill future positions by updating their job descriptions and hiring criteria.

Distribution and Shipping Centers

For a sizable mail- and online-order catalog company that distributes its merchandise from several centers in the Midwest, the picking is automated. However, there is a manual step where promotional inserts and catalogs are dropped into the box or bag. Their analysis uncovered a large Hispanic buyer base, and it didn't take them long to realize that those promotional offers and catalogs going into the packages would generate purchases if the inserts and catalogs going to Hispanic homes were in Spanish or were bilingual.

Retail Environment

As mentioned earlier, nowhere is it more important for employees to mirror customers than in a retail environment. Few things are more comforting or reassuring than to see a familiar face who possibly speaks one's language—at the bank, a favorite restaurant, the supermarket, the pharmacy, or the department store. This is true even among nonmulticultural consumers. Who doesn't like to be recognized by an acknowledging smile or even by name? This is one of the first areas companies should assess and optimize because people make choices on where they will shop based on whether familiar faces they trust work there.

While assessing the customer base for a major bank, I witnessed Asians, Hispanics, and African American customers waiting in line; every now and then, I'd see them allowing others to take their turn so they could be assisted by a specific teller who was of their same culture. It was amazing to me because presumably, we're all busy and want to be assisted as soon as possible. Yet these customers were willing to wait in line for someone who would make their experience more satisfying.

I have seen this behavior all over the country and in all types of retail businesses. Multicultural customers get in a specific line at the supermarket or the bank or sit in a specific section at a restaurant because they "like" the cashier or the teller or the server. But beyond the "like," they can identify with and communicate more comfortably and with greater confidence. I've even talked to customers who have switched to shop at a different location of the same store or switched to shopping at the competition because the person they were used to moved there or changed jobs.

While I was conducting ethnographies for a supermarket client, a Hispanic woman told me she had shopped at this supermarket chain for a long time, and while she used to shop at the location by her house, she now drives a little farther because the cashier she likes was transferred to the store where we were speaking. When I approached the cashier to hear her side of the story, she told me she'd been the only Hispanic working in the other store, and she felt more comfortable at her new store because there were two other Hispanic employees working there. Imagine if the "favorite" cashier had moved to the competition.

This is the power of creating a positive customer experience by optimizing the employee mix in retail locations. It's also important to consider the functions that support the retail environment, like web, social media, chat, and customer service at corporate.

Training and Development

When delivering on a strategy that is being expanded to satisfy a new market, a significant amount of communication is needed to support this direction. People can make or break any effort no matter how well it is planned and implemented. This means educating those involved in the implementation and those who are in the front lines about the new target market.

Education must include cultural-awareness and cultural-competency building for management and employees. It is impossible to staff the entire organization with multicultural employees. So those involved in the implementation must be educated and made to feel comfortable and familiar with the multicultural customers the company will target. They must understand the strategy and know what it will take to be successful, including the potential risks and rewards. Employees must be trained to feel vested in the strategy-expansion activity.

It's important to remind employees of the company's values and what they mean to the company and to the customers it serves. I recommend developing a statement for employees to use when a customer expresses concern over optimization activity that may be misinterpreted. Leadership should ensure every individual working for and with the company, including vendors, understands the company's position on hiring, developing, nurturing, and respecting the new targets and diverse employees.

A notable example of how top companies mobilize their organizations to understand, accept, and uphold a company's optimization efforts could be found in a CPG company whose commitment was impressive. Their goals included broadening individual awareness and strengthening their understanding of D&I, providing senior leaders with a broad perspective to inform the development of their D&I strategy, priorities, and tactics, and identifying practical next steps for beginning the D&I process.

They hired nine leading experts in the field of diversity and briefed them on the company's diversity goals. These experts traveled to company headquarters, where they rotated employees through company-wide presentations. These sessions were attended by the CEO, all leadership, including key leadership, and every headquarters employee. They discussed the business case for diversity and emphasized that this direction was not about being politically correct or meeting compliance requirements but rather a new direction that would improve shareholder value and the company's financial position. Every leader in each session was asked to write three to five short-term and midterm optimization changes they would make within the following thirty and ninety days. At the end of each day, the leaders and the CEO gathered to discuss in greater detail the work they would carry out over the next one to three months.

Marketing

Marketing to multicultural markets should be integrated into the CMO's responsibility and should be managed by senior and experienced marketing experts—the "A-Team." This is starting to happen in some organizations, but it's important to recognize that managing multicultural marketing activity is largely foreign to many senior marketers who have historically delegated the responsibility down or out of the organization to an agency partner.

Expanding the company's strategy to a new market to expand revenue flow and gain a future competitive advantage in the new market may be a vastly different frame from the one marketers may have adopted to date. Because general marketers lack deep multicultural-market expertise, they will need to become quick studies to gain an intimate understanding of their new market targets. Moreover, they will need to be very focused on supporting their company's strategies and established growth platforms while optimizing marketing execution to observe and acknowledge the new target's cultural nuances.

Marketers will need to be careful about the agency choices they make; they will need to rely on multicultural agency partners now more than ever.

This is critical. Just as the A-Team is assigned to carry out relevant delivery of the company's strategy to multicultural markets, so should you expect your agency partners to have proven expertise with these consumers. Ensure these agency relationships are productive for the company by developing top-level peer relationships with *all* your agencies and brief them on the business strategy and strategic insights required to produce work that will help expand the company's strategy successfully.

Agency relationships must be peer relationships rather than one agency overseeing or driving the direction of the other's work. There's nothing wrong with one agency providing leadership with the direction of the work, but they should not be managing the work being produced by smaller agencies. The CMO must commit to leading and providing feedback on the work.

Marketers will need to establish the KPIs and dashboards by which all marketing efforts will be measured and communicate these to their internal and external partners. They must also report multicultural sales and market-share gains results alongside core-target results.

Relevant Digital Presence

Multicultural consumers have a voracious appetite for anything digital. Because these consumers have long lived extremely social lives filled with family and friends, the fluidity of digital media is an effortless extension of their centuries-old cultural habits. Their devotion to friends and family means that success in the multicultural market won't come without an effective digital presence.

Marketers who integrate multicultural consumers into their digital story—to create and share—will have the most success creating meaningful relationships with these consumers online. This is a critical component when optimizing marketing through digital channels. Marketers should play an active role in multicultural conversations online regardless of the language while being mindful of the differences in cultural perspective and the type of value expectation consumers have relative to the language of the post.

A leading consumer-packaged baked-goods company took an active role in defining the role digital and social media could have in their current multimedia strategy targeting Hispanics. It conducted a thorough competitive assessment as well as listening exercises to see what the competition was doing and to hear how Hispanics engaged with these media in the context of their baking experiences. For several weeks, it assessed competitive activity for several competitors on their websites—Facebook, Twitter, Pinterest, Instagram, YouTube, and Google+—and were astounded by Hispanics' engagement. Recipes and social occasions differed from those used and preferred by non-Hispanic whites, and the company discovered that Latina food bloggers have tremendous influence. They had some optimizing and catching up to do as many of their competitors were already leveraging these insights and reflecting them across several platforms.

Today their websites in Spanish and English complement each other seamlessly yet feature unique occasions, promotions, and culturally relevant recipes in Spanish. Their tagline in Spanish not only reflects a sensitivity to the culture but also speaks relevantly to a younger generation, which was one important goal.

Modeling Organizational Readiness

One of the top three wireless companies had been targeting multicultural consumers for several years and had recently undergone a rotation of the leadership in charge of multicultural strategy. The new team felt it was important to benchmark the company's organizational readiness and moved to conduct a 360-degree assessment of touch points and the areas that supported them, including their Hispanic agency of record. The company's growth platform included increasing the penetration of smartphones and data plans across all targets, so the assessment work focused on ensuring the implementation maximized the company's ability to achieve this goal.

A geo-demographic analysis overlaying the client's customer data with Geoscape's demographics and acculturation model showed that many Hispanic clients living in Hispanic neighborhoods were closing contracts in stores in non-Hispanic neighborhoods. This meant that retail operations had to rethink staffing, digital strategy needed to rethink in-store digital assets, and merchandising needed to rethink signage in those stores. Internal planning meetings with respective departments were held to discuss a framework for defining store clusters and the appropriate merchandising, staffing, and digital-assets implementation for each.

It was also clear the company's marketing was misdirected. Millions of dollars were being allocated to media focused on very traditional programming and sponsorships because the company was primarily targeting Spanish-dominant Hispanics, and their own research said these consumers wanted primarily "talk and text" plans, not smartphones and data plans. Spanish-dominant customers were attracted by competitive "unlimited" offers for under $40, and this was far from the company's price range. While the media was successful in generating awareness and in-store efforts focused on selling them smartphones and data plans, these contracts were often short-lived because the customers would cancel their contracts within the first three months because of sticker shock. As a result, the sales analysis indicated that stores in neighborhoods with high Hispanic density had churn rates that were three times higher than the company average.

Bilingual and U.S.-born Hispanics, on the other hand, wanted smartphones and data plans and were willing to pay for them. Once the company understood the target and the alignment requirements were vetted by the respective areas and leadership, changes were made at corporate and at retail to align with the right target. The agency changed the target, and the media plan included some general-market media options for parts of their buy. Marketing facilitated the collaboration between general-market and Hispanic agencies so the client's business and marketing objectives could be more precisely executed.

Organizational readiness is crucial for success. Optimizing important implementation areas isn't difficult. Companies have the internal experts who know what to do and how to do it. They just need to expand their implementation thinking to include a new market—the multicultural targets that make sense for them. It does require doing the work I've described. And more importantly, it requires collective involvement and participation from those responsible for implementation. Organizational readiness helps companies deliver their strategies relevantly and has the power to increase revenue streams.

Chapter 10

The Long View

By now, it should be clear that while revenue-growth potential exists internationally, equally significant revenue-growth potential exists domestically, and expanding company strategies to multicultural markets represents a tremendous top-line opportunity for companies looking for sustained future growth. The multicultural market right here at home has the potential to help many businesses survive tough times and thrive during periods of economic strength while providing a considerable competitive edge. Yes, it will require a reframing of how this new consumer market fits within company goals and strategies, perhaps the need to adopt a broader and future-minded perspective, perhaps objective consideration of the current and future economic value at stake, perhaps a complete revamping of current multicultural practices.

One thing is sure: multicultural market success is not easy, and it doesn't happen overnight. Entering a new market, even when you're "just" expanding an existing strategy, requires a one-to-three-year outlook. That means patience, and it also means putting your best foot forward to position your company for that future-ready state.

The reframing and mind-set shifts described in Chapters 5 through 9 are meant to help reinforce what you already know—that entering a new market requires disciplined analysis and planning, organizing to relevantly deliver the company's strategy, and allocating the appropriate resources to get the job done. This chapter shares a few more areas that require attention and consideration. It discusses what is required to gain internal traction, budget-allocation considerations, and practices that help ensure sustainability. It ends with a case study that I believe demonstrates modeling a commitment to future revenue growth and value building.

Creating Your Own Best Practices

As companies organize for multicultural market success, they usually want to know about other companies that are "doing it right and how they are doing it." I believe that best practices can provide valuable benchmarks for a company's new efforts to target multicultural consumers. Best practices are especially helpful to companies that are targeting a new market for the first time because those best practices are likely the results of several rounds of test-and-learn efforts. This can save valuable resources as well as time during ramp-up.

However, it's also important to be cautious about putting too much weight on another company's best practices because each company's goals, strategies, and market situations are unique. No company is the mirror image of another. Even within the same industry, different companies have different corporate cultures, different market positions, and different business priorities, which can make their best practices ineffective, inefficient, and even completely irrelevant. Best practices are always in the eye of the beholder. On the surface, it may seem as though a company's best practices are generating success for them, yet they may be facing just as many challenges. Consider that when companies' successes, case studies, or conference presentations are shared publicly, they typically highlight the positives, and the missteps, the trial and error, the shortfalls, and even the resistance or lack of implementation support faced internally are generally absent.

Just as important is how well or enthusiastically stakeholders will be about adopting an external best practice. In my experience, internal stakeholders are seldom as engaged or committed to adopting, implementing, and ensuring the sustainability of best practices they've had a minimal role in creating. They are much more likely to support applications that consider their input and have been vetted against the day-to-day reality of their functions, responsibilities, and challenges.

Though it can be tempting to look for the "best" solution externally, it doesn't always work. I've encountered countless examples of teams that travel to large multicultural markets where they believe the competition is "doing it right." However, they have adopted certain best practices that are completely inappropriate for their companies and for their multicultural consumers. In such cases, the results don't pan out as expected, money and resources are wasted, and it leaves many of these companies feeling less than motivated to try again.

As you organize to expand your strategy to a new market, don't look for shortcuts or cookie-cutter approaches. Rather, be observant and do the due diligence. Go ahead and discuss best practices in roundtables with marketers who may have more experience targeting multicultural markets but use these observations and conversations as a basis for further thought about whether what you hear is relevant to your company, products, and the customers you're trying to attract. I encourage revisiting existing best practices that are already successful within your organization and give some thought as to how they might be optimized to better satisfy your multicultural targets. You'll find the alignment work will be minor and the best practices will be a better fit for your company (specific business situations, goals, existing strategies, operations, and infrastructure). That commitment to your company's culture and organization will make your efforts more relevant and consistent with your own business practices.

Harnessing Intellectual Capital

Knowledge management is challenging for companies on many levels. In the case of multicultural market knowledge, companies often invest hundreds of thousands of dollars to create and protect intellectual capital because it is an increasingly important source of competitive advantage.

However, maintaining this intellectual capital can be challenging for client organizations because information and data on their multicultural targets are often collected and analyzed outside of the organization by an agency partner or by the company's multicultural manager, who often lacks cross-functional support from data-analytics, market-research, and insights teams. As a result, the data and the knowledge it provides often disappear when the person in charge leaves the company or is transferred out of multicultural units or when the company's advertising work moves to another ad agency. To add to this instability, as multicultural units are dissolved, internal multicultural experts who leave or who are integrated into brand teams may be reluctant to voluntarily share the hard-earned insights because they represent leverage when their companies are reorganizing or "right-sizing" operations and the people in them. This leaves the company with no foundation of multicultural knowledge and the precarious situation of having no intellectual capital to gain a competitive advantage. Every time this happens, the company must build its knowledge from scratch.

In the new future-minded paradigm, which seeks to attain a position of competitive advantage in multicultural markets, processes for formally maintaining knowledge must be created and managed as part of the big picture. Companies must give some thought to how modern technologies, internal functions, and leaders can form a symbiotic relationship to capture and synthesize information that can be available to share as needed by those in charge of expansion implementation and management.

Multicultural Assets

As companies seek to become increasingly diverse, the insights that come from diverse employees are invaluable. However, it is important to temper the excitement and expectation that these individuals have all the answers, especially if they've been previously assigned responsibility for managing multicultural activity. One person or even a small group of people of a certain culture do not represent all the attitudes and behaviors of their culture. Having diverse employees enhances the company's ability to understand, put in proper context, and consider different views and opinions from which different and valuable ideas and concepts can be generated, but these views and opinions are based on limited experiences.

Consider that multicultural executives, while having a range of experiences with their culture, have also been schooled to think in more Americanized ways, which may not be entirely representative of the cultures from which they come. As such, companies must be careful not to place too much weight on one person or a group of people (as in ERGs) when attempting to assess the relative value of an idea, a concept, or a product among a target segment, even when they belong to that segment of the population.

It is also a mistake to test important ideas, concepts, or products among your company employees, including administrative assistants, cafeteria staff, factory floor workers, or maintenance crews. These individuals likely do not meet the specific target profiles and are likely to be positively biased so they can ingratiate themselves with the person—typically an executive—asking the questions. And again, these individuals are not representative of the target market. While bilingual employees are valuable for creating relevance for your products and services across customer touch points, they cannot possibly compensate for operational gaps the company has not addressed in its implementation any more than any other employee would be able to compensate for gaps in strategy delivery among non-Hispanic white customers. Depending on such unrealistic expectations will not be productive.

Making decisions based on ad hoc research is risky because the feedback may not represent the true potential of the idea being tested. Companies must invest in proper market research using experienced vendors so the insights can drive valuable decisions that will result in competitive advantage. When the expansion team defines crucial strategy-delivery areas that will support revenue generation, only seamless and relevant implementation based on solid market research will succeed in engaging multicultural targets and growing sales.

Allocating Resources

Thinking back to the Three Horizons Framework discussed in Chapter 5, Horizon Two aims to position a company advantageously for future growth in a growing market or geography by expanding its existing strategy to a new market, thereby capturing a new revenue stream. This requires investment commensurate to the task. It requires resources for new business-building capabilities. It requires solid and sustained investment to deliver the strategy relevantly and holistically.

The apprehension many managers feel when making budget-allocation decisions is based on rapid ROI expectations, which isn't unusual given the short-term mind-set most business-unit leaders have when they are focused on Horizon One activity. However, evaluating the value of an investment to expand into a new market based on ROI is premature. ROI measures the efficiency of an investment and the return on an investment, but entry strategies, by their very nature, will evolve and will impact return efficiency.

Instead, when entering a new market, a company's economic metrics should focus on top-line growth (revenue), sales velocity, market share, and NPV, which looks at the cash flow from the investment in the present and the predicted future cash flow. As such, allocating robust budgets to a new market entry requires significant CEO oversight and an empowered senior leader with an entrepreneurial spirit and business-building skills who can effectively defend budgets from larger "bread and butter" core activities.

In this sense, one might say that larger companies have internal as well as external competition, and internal competition for funding can be fierce. This is the reason CEO involvement is so necessary to adequately fund Horizon Two activity. The CEO needs to be able to greenlight additional funding by shutting down or cutting investments in other areas to fund strategy-expansion activity when it makes sense.

Appropriate funding is critical to success for a variety of reasons, including these:

- The ability to attract star talent to lead and manage the initiative. These hires need direct report lines to the C-suite to protect the activity and incentives for achieving milestones.
- The investment to produce revenue results quickly relative to other company initiatives. Results need to be significant and quick enough to matter with the goal of leading management to reprioritize other initiatives in its favor if necessary.

The allocation of time, people, money, and other resources is always a concern for companies that target multicultural consumers. Budgets are reportedly already spread too thin and focused on achieving the goals of Horizon One core activity. As a result, funding for multicultural market activity—a Horizon Two effort—has been historically arbitrary and inconsistent and therefore often produces inconsistent results or no results at all. Reframing the investment allocation as a Horizon Two investment is critical to shifting the activity's importance vis-à-vis how it is perceived today. In the new paradigm, CEOs see that expanding their company's strategy to a new market of category users by targeting high-value multicultural consumers is a growth priority for the future that requires investment proportionate to the task.

Gaining Traction

Gaining internal traction is perhaps the single largest barrier when companies decide to target multicultural segments. This stems from the dynamics currently in play (as discussed in Chapters 3 and 4). It's unlikely the organization will be compelled to properly allocate its people, time, and budget in support under the following circumstances: when the role that multicultural segments play in the company's growth trajectory is unclear, when the market expansion is not being explained and managed at a level commensurate to its importance to the company's present and future revenue goals, when the activity is not integrated, and when leaders are not held accountable for results.

Internal competition for resources is severe. Managers are usually focused on defending, extending, and increasing the profitability of existing businesses. Managers focused on Horizon One activity seldom want anything to do with an activity that may disrupt their processes and implementation unless a senior executive has given them solid reasons and no choice but to do so. Therefore, C-suite leadership and commitment is crucial. Without it, efforts to expand the delivery of the company's strategy to a new market effectively will be futile.

A plan that lays out the budget, time frame, milestones, and metrics that focus on revenue and NPV should be communicated to the leadership team and to the required functional areas. Then as the expansion efforts begin to produce results, it's important to have the infrastructure in place to collect the data so it can be analyzed to demonstrate progress and successes.

All four executives highlighted in Chapter 2 have successfully led strategy expansions for their companies, and all four speak of their dependence on data to provide both the business case as well as proof of the expansion's economic value to the company. Some even use their data as inputs to projection models, which, along with other variables such as population growth, serve as powerful proofs of concept in the present and into the future. These executives would tell you that nothing helps strengthen internal support better than objective data. Even the toughest skeptics cannot deny the power of what data reveals.

How the Long View Worked for One Company

There are companies where the leadership was not years but decades ahead of their time. They saw the future and organized to capitalize on it. These early adopters were innovators in this realm and helped catapult their organizations into multicultural market leadership.

One such example is Jim Kilts, who headed the $27 billion Worldwide Food group (Kraft Foods) of Philip Morris as executive vice president from 1994 to 1997. In that role, Kilts was responsible for integrating Kraft and General Foods worldwide and for shaping the group's domestic and international strategy and plans. Jim is one of the most renowned turnaround CEOs in corporate America.

In the early 1990s, Kilts insisted on the development of a strategy to grow market share among U.S. Hispanics, African Americans, and Asians for the portfolio of Kraft brands. He appointed his top people to assess the company's ability to move in this direction. When they said it couldn't work at Kraft because of the way the company was structured and because of the corporate culture, Kilts insisted his leadership team develop a strategy to mobilize the entire Kraft organization toward this goal. Kilts made ethnic marketing an imperative for all his division presidents, and the presidents conveyed the mandate to the brand teams. Top-level individuals were assigned to manage the strategy alongside the brand teams. An ethnic marketing shadow P&L was created and managed by the ethnic marketing group. All the divisions were required to allocate budgets to the ethnic marketing group budget based on brand-development positions and market-share growth goals.

Kraft Foods pioneered the work with Nielsen to develop the measurement model to read Hispanic share and volume for the brand groups and retail accounts. Kraft hired four Hispanic agencies (three regional promotional agencies to support retail programs and one national branding AOR), and they were required to collaborate. The agencies were included in telephone and in-person meetings with the brand teams and participated in weekly strategic-planning video-conference calls during brand-plan development periods. Additionally, one of the first examples of processes for cross-functional support was implemented at Kraft Foods; it included allocating a point person and support for the ethnic marketing group from market research, the Kraft kitchens, strategy, promotions, and the photography studio (to name a few).

Sales teams collaborated with the agencies and provided input on key account needs and challenges. Sales teams were trained on how to sell ethnic-market retail-program overlays for key drive periods to customer accounts and would bring an agency representative for support and credibility building as needed.

Kraft succeeded in growing market share and volume for most of its brands and achieved tremendous credibility and respect among retail customers. Kraft Foods is a successful pioneer in ethnic marketing and is considered one of the best examples in CPGs.

Future Success Requires Sustained Commitment

It's clear that successfully expanding a company's strategy delivery to a new target requires a CEO who sees the new market's future revenue-growth potential and demonstrates focused commitment.

Sustained success will require the following:

- Assignment of high-level leadership to lead and manage the activity—the "A-Team"
- Hands-on management rather than delegation of the strategy-expansion effort to internal and external multicultural experts
- Integration into the company's goal-setting and strategic-planning process
- Relevant strategy delivery through optimized implementation efforts
- Acknowledgement that building revenue in a new market requires the same amount of time and money as it does to build revenue for any new and future oriented initiative

As American companies evolve their views and reframe the role of multicultural targets in their efforts to grow revenue, the benefits of multicultural population growth and spending power will prove rewarding. For many companies, it already has.

Pursuing new markets will require that companies do some deep thinking about the internal adjustments required rather than relying on what they see others doing. The truth is that with minimal adjustments, many company best practices will serve them well in their pursuit of new markets if they understand how to apply them.

Knowing how to apply a company's proven practices requires learning about new markets through traditional market research. There are no shortcuts to the required groundwork to understand a new market, and this knowledge must be shared with key implementers while also protected as valuable intellectual property.

Funding and managing expansion implementation will require leadership involvement that works to ensure its viability and sustainability as the expansion takes hold. Gaining traction for a new initiative, especially when it requires significant investment for which other initiatives will compete, may be difficult. As such, leadership must work to ensure that those in charge of Horizon One activity understand the role and importance of Horizon Two activity to the company's future growth, especially as the country's demographics and buying power continue to shift. I propose this approach to growing revenue among multicultural markets because I know the benefits can be substantial for any company that sets out to expand their market strategies in a disciplined, properly managed, well-integrated, and well-funded manner.

Appendix: Resources

Consultants with Multicultural Market Expertise

Davila Multicultural Insights
16101 Ventura Blvd., Suite 315
Encino, CA 91436
818.285.8729
http://www.davilami.com/

New Majority Consulting
12920 SE 38th St.
Bellevue, WA 98006
425.867.9087

Santiago Solutions Group
300 E. Oakland Park Blvd., Suite 361
Wilton Manors, FL 33334
818.509.5901
http://santiagosolutionsgroup.com/

Market Research and Data Companies with Multicultural Market Expertise

Collage Group / Latinum Network
2 Bethesda Metro Center, Suite 300
Bethesda, MD 20814

240.482.8260
http://www.collagegroup.com/

Garcia Research
74390 Zeppelin Dr.
Palm Desert, CA 92211
323.376.3622
www.garciaresearchops.com

Geoscape
1395 Coral Way
Miami, FL 33145
305.860.1460
http://geoscape.com/

GfK Research
300 E. Magnolia Blvd., Suite 400
Burbank, CA 91506
818.276.9102
http://www.gfk.com/en-us

New American Dimensions
6955 La Tijera Blvd., Suite B
Los Angeles, CA 90045
310.670.6800
http://www.newamericandimensions.com/

Nielsen
85 Broad St.
New York, NY 10004
800.864.1224
http://www.nielsen.com/us/en.html

NPD Group Inc.
900 W. Shore Rd.
Port Washington, NY 11050
516.625.0700

http://www.npd.com

ORC International
229 W. 43rd St., 8th Floor
New York, NY 10036
212.645.4500
https://orcinternational.com/

Packaged Facts
11200 Rockville Pike,
Suite 504
Rockville, MD 20852
800.298.5294
https://www.packagedfacts.com/

Pew Hispanic Center
1615 L. St., NW, Suite 800
Washington, DC 20036-5610
202.419.4300
http://www.pewresearch.org/

Scarborough Research
85 Broad St.
New York, NY 10004
800.864.1224
http://www.nielsen.com/us/en/solutions/capabilities/scarborough-local.
html

Simmons Market Research
800 Fairway Dr., Suite 295
Deerfield Beach, FL 33441
800.551.6425
http://www.simmonssurvey.com/

Spectra Research
589 Congress Park Drive
Dayton, OH 45459

937.320.5999
http://www.spectra-research.com/

Synovate Americas
16133 Ventura Blvd., Suite 1000
Encino, CA 91436
818.380.1480
http://www.synovate.com/

The Selig Center for Economic Growth
Terry College of Business,
University of Georgia
600 South Lumpkin St.
Athens, GA 30622
706.542.8100
http://www.terry.uga.edu/about/centers-institutes/selig

ThinkNow Research
2100 W. Magnolia Blvd., Suite A/B
Burbank, CA 91506
818.843.0220
https://thinknowresearch.com/

Government Agencies with Demographic Data

Bureau of Labor Statistics (BLS)
Postal Square Building
2 Massachusetts Ave. NE
Washington, DC 20212
202.691.5200
http://stats.bls.gov

U.S. Department of Commerce
1401 Constitution Ave. NW
Washington, DC 20230
202.482.4883
http://www.doc.gov

U.S. Census Bureau
4700 Silver Hill Road
Washington, DC 20233-0001
818.267.1700
www.census.gov/

Multicultural Industry Associations

Association of Hispanic Advertising Agencies (AHAA)
8201 Greensboro Dr., Suite 300
McLean, VA 22102
703.610.9014

Association National Advertisers (ANA)
708 Third Ave., 33rd Floor
New York, NY 10017
212.697.5950
http://www.ana.net/committee/profile/id/MULTI

National Association of Asian American Professionals
4850 Sugarloaf Parkway, Suite 209-289
Lawrenceville, GA 30044
919.625.1207
http://www.naaap.org/

National Black MBA Association
400 W. Peachtree NW, Suite 203
Atlanta, GA 30308
404.260.5444
https://nbmbaa.org/

PROHISPANICA (previously National Society of Hispanic MBAs
— NSHMBA)
1303 Walnut Hill Lane, Suite 300
Irving, TX 75038
214.596.9338
http://www.nshmba.org/

Bibliography

Acosta and Univision
The Why? Behind the Buy
https://www.independentagent.com/Resources/StaffDevelopment/
Diversity/Pages/ARG/Hispanic/4th-Edition-Hispanic-The-Why-Behind-
The-Buy.pdf

AdvertisingAge
14th Annual Hispanic Fact Pack, 2017
http://adage.com/trend-reports/report.php?id=119

AdvertisingAge
Leading National Advertisers Fact Pack
http://adage.com/d/resources/resources/
whitepaper/200-leading-national-advertisers-2017-fact-pack

Aftermarket Business World
2017 Aftermarket Business World Hispanic Consumer Attitude Study
http://images2.advanstar.com/PixelMags/amb/digitaledition/11-2017.
html#16

AHAA (courtesy of Santiago Solutions Group)
Hispanic Ad Allocation Impact on Revenue Growth Study Series: Parts
I–III
http://santiagosolutionsgroup.com/
ahaa-study-2011-advertising-budget-alignment-october-2011/

AHAA (courtesy of Santiago Solutions Group)
Hispanic Ad Spend Allocation Trends 2006–2014
What Impact Has It Delivered Marketers? Where Do We Go from Here?

Atlanta Black Star
Black Buying Power Has Reached Tipping Point, But How Will Black
America Leverage It to Create Wealth?
http://atlantablackstar.com/2016/02/04/2016-nielsen-report-black-
buying-power-reached-tipping-point-will-black-america-leverage-create-
wealth/

Automotive Digest and CNW Research
Retail Automotive Summary
http://automotivedigest.com/wp-content/uploads/2013/08/Retail-
Automotive-Summary-August-2013.pdf

Brown, Jennifer. *Inclusion*. Driven Purpose Publishing, 2017.

Baghai, Mehrdad, Stephen Coley, and David White. *The Alchemy of
Growth: Practical Insights for Building an Enduring Enterprise*. Basic
Books, May 2000.CMO Council
Activating the New American Mainstream
https://www.cmocouncil.org/thought-leadership/reports/301/download

Collage/Latinum Network
The Big Shift: Understanding the Importance of Multicultural
Consumers in the U.S. Economy
http://info.collagegroup.com/
hispanic-multicultural-market-opportunity-spending-shifts

Convenience Store News
Hispanic Population Growth Helps Fuel Financial Services
https://csnews.com/
hispanic-population-growth-helps-fuel-financial-services

Dealer Marketing Magazine
How Dealers Can Reach the Underserved Hispanic Market

http://www.dealermarketing.com/
how-dealers-can-reach-the-underserved-hispanic-market/

Deloite Insights
Diversity as an Engine of Innovation
https://www2.deloitte.com/insights/us/en/deloitte-review/issue-8/
diversity-as-an-engine-of-innovation.html

Frey, William H. *Diversity Explosion How New Racial Demographics Are Remaking America*. Brookings Institution, November 2014.

Geoscape
Cumulative Lifetime Spending, pages 51–60
AMDS 2017 Executive Summary Report

Harvard University Library Open Collections Program
Aspiration, Acculturation and Impact
Immigration to the United States, 1789–1930
http://ocp.hul.harvard.edu/immigration/goldrush.html

History.com
Slavery in America
https://www.history.com/topics/black-history/slavery

History.com
U.S. Immigration before 1965
https://www.history.com/topics/u-s-immigration-before-1965

Interview with Mark Stockdale, former VP of Multicultural Marketing for T-Mobile

Interview with Angel Colón, Senior Director, Diversity, Multicultural Development, and Supplier Diversity for Kroger Co.

Interview with Lisa Kranc, former Senior Vice President of Marketing for AutoZone

Interview with Russell A. Bennett, former Vice President of Opportunity Strategy and Development and Latino Solutions for UnitedHealthcare Group

Interview with Peter Francese, Advisor and Principal of the New England Consulting Group and Founder of *American Demographics* Magazine

Interview with Gloria Tostado, former Multicultural Marketing Executive for Verizon Wireless, Harris Bank, and Circuit City

Conversation with Johanna Marolf, former Director of Latino Connections at H&R Block

Conversation with Carlos Santiago at Santiago Solutions Group

Conversation with Cesar Melgoza at Geoscape

Conversation with Bryan Garcia, Account Planner Extraordinaire at Conill Advertising

Conversation with David Wellisch at Collage Group/Latinum Network

Conversation with Gilbert Davila at Davila Multicultural Insights and Chair of ANA Multicultural Committee

Conversation with Luis Nieto, retired President of Consumer Products at ConAgra, past President of Refrigerated Products at Dean Foods, past President at Federated Group, and past SVP at Kraft Foods

Latino Decisions for W. K. Kellogg Foundation
The State of the Latino Family — National Survey of Latinos
http://www.latinodecisions.com/files/2114/1599/5051/Exec_Summary_WKKF_State_of_the_Latino_Family_2014.pdf

McKinsey & Company
Diversity Matters, February 2, 2015

https://www.mckinsey.com/~/media/mckinsey/business%20
functions/organization/our%20insights/why%20diversity%20matters/
diversity%20matters.ashx

Migration Policy Institute
Asian Immigrants in the United States
https://www.migrationpolicy.org/article/asian-immigrants-united-states

Migration Policy Institute
Frequently Requested Statistics on Immigrants and Immigration in the
United States, February 2018
https://www.migrationpolicy.org/article/
frequently-requested-statistics-immigrants-and-immigration-united-states

Nielsen
The Multicultural Edge: Rising Super Consumers
http://www.nielsen.com/us/en/insights/reports/2015/the-multicultural-
edge-rising-super-consumers.html

Nielsen
Hispanic Influence Reaches New Heights in the U.S.
http://www.nielsen.com/us/en/insights/news/2016/hispanic-influence-
reaches-new-heights-in-the-us.html

Nielsen
From the Ballot to the Grocery Store: A 2016 Perspective on Growing
Hispanic Influence in America
http://www.ethnifacts.com/nielsen-hispanics-consumer-report-
august-2016.pdf

Nielsen
Increasingly Affluent, Educated and Diverse African-American
Consumers: The Untold Story (2015 Report)
http://www.nielsen.com/content/dam/corporate/us/en/reports-
downloads/2015-reports/african-american-consumer-untold-story-
sept-2015.pdf

Nielsen
Asian-Americans: Culturally Diverse and Expanding Their Footprint
http://nielsencommunity.com/report_files/Asian_Consumer_
Report_2016_Final.pdf

Nielsen
Multicultural Millennials: The Multiplier Effect
http://www.nielsen.com/us/en/insights/reports/2017/multicultural-
millennials--the-multiplier-effect.html

Package Facts
Hispanics: Demographic and Consumer Spending Trends, 9th Edition
https://www.packagedfacts.com/
Hispanics-Demographic-Consumer-10124772/

Packaged Facts
Latino Food Shoppers Increasingly Mirror Habits of American
Consumers Overall
https://www.packagedfacts.com/about/release.asp?id=3611

Pew Research Center
Multiracial in America: Proud, Diverse and Growing in Numbers
http://www.pewsocialtrends.org/2015/06/11/multiracial-in-america/

Pew Research Center
The Hispanic Population Growth Has Leveled Off
http://www.pewresearch.org/
fact-tank/2017/08/03/u-s-hispanic-population-growth-has-leveled-off/

Pew Research Center
Key Findings about U.S. immigrants
http://www.pewresearch.org/fact-tank/2017/05/03/
key-findings-about-u-s-immigrants/

Pew Research
Afro-Latino: A Deeply Rooted Identity among U.S. Hispanics

http://www.pewresearch.org/fact-tank/2016/03/01/
afro-latino-a-deeply-rooted-identity-among-u-s-hispanics/

Pew Research Center
It's Official: Minority Babies Are the Majority among the Nation's
Infants, but Only Just
http://www.pewresearch.org/fact-tank/2016/06/23/its-official-minority-
babies-are-the-majority-among-the-nations-infants-but-only-just/

Pew Research Center
Future Immigration Will Change the Face of America by 2065
http://www.pewresearch.org/fact-tank/2015/10/05/
future-immigration-will-change-the-face-of-america-by-2065/

Population Reference Bureau
Population Bulletin Aging in the United States, December 2015
https://assets.prb.org/pdf16/aging-us-population-bulletin.pdf

Porter, Michael E. *Competitive Strategy.* Free Press, 1998.

Prudential
The Hispanic American Financial Experience, 2014
https://www.prudential.com/media/managed/hispanic_en/
prudential_hafe_researchstudy_2014_en.pdf

PWC
20th CEO Survey U.S. Business Leadership in the World in 2017
https://www.pwc.com/gx/en/ceo-survey/pdf/20th-global-ceo-survey-us-
supplement-executive-dialogues.pdf

Retailwire.com
The Growth Solution — Strategic Relevance
https://www.retailwire.com/page/1/?s=soto

Selig Center for Economic Growth, Terry College of Business, University
of Georgia

Multicultural Economy Report, 2017
http://www.terry.uga.edu/about/centers-institutes/selig/publications

The Journal of Economic History
The Rise and Fall of Indentured Servitude in the Americas: An
Economic Analysis
https://www.colorado.edu/ibs/es/alston/econ8534/SectionIII/Galenson,_
The_Rise_and_Fall_of_Indentured_Servitude_in_the_
Americas.pdf

The Hill
Aging White Population Speeding Diversity
http://thehill.com/homenews/news/308357-decline-of-americas-white-
population-accelerating-study-finds

The Shelby Report
The Multicultural Economy
http://www.theshelbyreport.com/2011/10/28/the-multicultural-economy/

The Six Laws of Customer Experience, Bruce Temkin
https://experiencematters.files.wordpress.com/2008/07/
the-6-laws-of-customer-experience_v4.pdf

University of Georgia
Minority Groups Driving U.S. Economy
https://news.uga.edu/Multicultural-economy-report-17/

Univision
Hispanic Impact on Wireless Growth, October 2017

Univision
U.S. Hispanic Millennials: Portraits of a Mobile-First Generation, 2017

Univision
Winning with Hispanics, October 2017

Univision
Banking on Hispanics for Growth, November 2017

Univision
Hispanics and Groceries, 2017Univision
Hispanic Nutrition Insights, May 2017

Univision
Hispanics and Health Insurance, September 2017

Univision
Hispanics and Entertainment, June 2017

Univision
The Hispanic Electronics Consumer, October 2017

U.S. Census Bureau
U.S. Race and Ethnic Profiles by Age Groups, 2015

U.S. Census Bureau
A Look at the U.S. Population in 2060
https://www.census.gov/newsroom/cspan/pop_proj/20121214_cspan_
popproj.pdf

U.S. Census Bureau
New Census Bureau Report Analyzes U.S. Population Projections,
March 2015
https://www.census.gov/newsroom/press-releases/2015/cb15-tps16.html

U.S. Bureau of Labor Statistics
Consumer Expenditure Survey, August 2017
About Marketing Solutions Inc. Analysis
https://www.bls.gov/cex/2015/combined/age.pdf

Index

Americans, xii, 3, 6–7, 10, 13
American standards, 40
ANA (Association of National Advertisers), 72, 155
analysts, 11, 22
analytics, 29, 123
ancestries, 6
annual growth rates, 23
anti-immigrant sentiment, xiii
anti-immigrant stance, 81
apparel, 16, 33–36
appreciate, xii–xiv, 18, 52, 73, 99
appreciation, xii–xiv, 74, 88–89, 91, 95, 101
apprehensions, 42, 46, 145
arbitrary resource allocations, 74
archetypes, 51–52, 55–56
Arizona, 10
ARPU (average revenue per unit), 25
Asian Americans, 155
Asian buying power, 11–12, 21
Asian market spending, 50, 61
Asian-owned firms, 13
assessment
  360-degree, 24, 139
  competitive, 24, 139
assimilate, 3
AT&T, 57, 112
attitudes, 3, 8, 85–87, 89, 108, 110, 144
audio-visual equipment and services, 23
authenticity, 39
auto aftermarket, 28, 30
auto insurance, 34
AutoZone, xvii, 28–29
average American, 13, 82
average consumers, xi, 26, 82–83
average revenue, 25

B

B2B (business-to-business), 43, 123–24
B2C (business-to-consumer), 43, 123
back-end operations, 50, 61, 126

backlash, 80–81
Baghai, Mehrdad, xv, 76
benchmark, 49–50, 108, 139, 142
Bennett, Russell A., x, xvii, 30–32, 47
best practices, 55, 108, 142–43, 150
Bezos, Jeff, 75, 81
big market change, 53
birth rates, 2, 4, 11, 41
BLS (Bureau of Labor Statistics), 16–17, 19, 22, 30, 34–37
boomer generation, 2, 83
bottom-line value, 38
brand development, 24
brand-implementation plans, 79
brand penetration, 74–75
break even, 21, 40
BRIC (Brazil, Russia, India, and China), 21
budget, xiv, 26, 37–38, 42, 44–45, 47, 50–51, 55, 58, 60, 68–70, 72, 79, 118, 146–48
budget allocation, 37, 50–51, 70
budget-allocation criteria, 61
budget efficiencies, 51
budget flexibility, 114
budget limitations, 44
Buffett, Warren, 81
Burger King, 69
business-building skills, 45, 146
business case, 44, 69, 102, 106
business director, 62
business enterprise, 73
business-model effectiveness, 73
business models, xiii–xiv, 50, 60, 74, 117, 127
business performance, 100–101, 122
business practices, x, 143
business priorities, 59, 142
business process, x
business propositions, 52

business strategy, xi, 8–9, 20, 40, 91, 96, 114, 119, 127, 138

business units, 30, 59, 71, 79, 105, 120, 127

business-unit vice president, 62

buying power, xi, 7, 9–13, 21, 150

C

CAGR (compound annual growth rate), 26–27

California, 10, 12

California Gold Rush, 5

call metrics, 86

capabilities, 74–75, 102, 114, 117–18, 133

capturing, xi, 18, 20, 23, 47, 145

car sales, 29

case studies, 55, 142

cash flow, 76–77, 79, 116, 146

category consumer expenditures, 17

category development, 64

category-growth strategies, 105

category users, 64, 115, 126, 147

cell service, 33

Central Americans, 9

CEO (chief executive officer), ix, xiii, 38–40, 45, 81, 99, 104, 107, 109–11, 114, 124, 127, 137, 146–47, 149

CEO involvement, 57, 146

champions, 8, 38, 74

change, xii, xiv, 7, 52–53, 73, 78, 82, 91, 96, 100–102, 107–8, 110–11, 118, 127

Chesky, Brian, 81

Chiat/Day, 69–70

children's apparel, 33

Chinese, 11–12

Chinese Asians, 5

clarity, 90, 114

  accountability, 116

C-suite, 114

  decision, 115

  integration, 116

  metrics, 116

  optimization, 116

  organizational, 114

  strategic, 114

  target, 115

  value, 115

client-side consolidation, 72

CMO Council survey, 44, 48, 50

Coca-Cola, 22, 27, 56

Cold War, 5

Coley, Stephen, xv, 76

Collage Group, xvii, 22

collective unconscious, 51

college attendance, 14

college education, 11, 14, 69, 85

Colón, Angel, xvii, 26–27, 48

Colorado, 10

Comcast, 57

comfort zones, 8

commitment, 62, 74, 91, 99, 112, 136, 142–43, 147, 149

committed archetypes, 56

committed companies, 27, 37, 57

committed leaders, 56

common denominator, 55

communication, xiv, 49, 64–65, 69, 85, 98–99, 109, 122, 129–31, 136

communication divide, 64

community, xii–xiii, 59, 74, 86, 102

company direction, 62

company stakeholders, 28

company values, 93

company-wide integration, 68

comparative expense analysis, 31

competency training, 60, 107

competing priorities, 44–45

competitive advantage, 7, 74, 113–15, 132, 137, 143–45

competitive differentiator, 102
competitive positioning, 102
competitive structure, 41
computers, 23
ConAgra Consumer Products, xvii
Conill Advertising, xvii, 160
conservative views, 80
consolidation, 69, 72
consumer characteristics, 130
consumer confidence, xi
Consumer Expenditure Survey, 30, 33, 35
consumer segments, 62, 129
consumer spending increases, 18
consumption, 3, 15, 23, 37, 40–41, 46, 48, 59, 61, 64, 77
consumption habits, 3
Cook, Tim, 81
coordinated efforts, 38
core business, 45, 76, 79, 115–16
core competency, xiv, 68
core consumers, 45
core customers, 43, 45, 53, 80, 82
core markets, 55, 82–83
core-market share, 82
corporate America, xi, 52, 54–55, 66, 91, 148
corporate culture, 52, 90–91, 93, 99, 102, 142, 148
corporate headquarters, 100
correlation analysis, 37
cost reduction, 39
counterintuitive, 43, 53
counterparts, 15
counterproductive, 54, 63
course-corrected, 27
CPG (consumer packaged goods), 27–28, 38, 108, 149
creative work, 59
credit card usage, 23
critical differentiators, 33

critical success factor, 40
cross-business-line participation, 121
cross-functional areas, 25, 57, 121, 143, 149
cross-functional responsibility, 57
C-suite, xiv, 44, 65, 91, 94, 101, 105, 107, 110–11, 146
Cubans, 9–10
cultural appreciation, 3, 8, 89, 91, 95, 101
cultural awareness, 44, 46, 91–92, 97, 102, 104, 107
cultural-awareness and cultural-competency training, 86
cultural backgrounds, 8, 72, 95, 99
cultural change, 7, 78, 102
cultural competence, 122
cultural competency, xiv, 72, 74, 91–92, 99, 102, 117
cultural development, 46
cultural differences, 92, 101, 107
cultural evolution, 2
cultural fluency, 100
cultural inclinations, 26
cultural intelligence, xiv–xv, 4, 40, 46, 62, 73, 110
culturally competent, x, 53, 116, 119
cultural nuances, 8, 46, 137
cultural profiles, 2, 97
cultural understanding, 97
cumulative lifetime spending, 18
cumulative shareholder value, 37
customer centricity, 93
customer-centric myth, 92
customer-centric values, 52
customer experiences, 8, 32, 49–50, 52, 63, 74, 89, 92, 95, 106, 129
customer lifetime value, 15
customer preferences, 29, 101
customer services, 130, 134, 136
customer touch points, 61, 145
cutback strategies, 39

D

dabblers archetype, 52, 55–56
DACA (Deferred Action for Childhood Arrivals Act or Dreamers Act, 81
dashboards (KPI), 25, 138
data analytics, 128
Davila, Gilbert, xvii
Davila Multicultural Insights, xvii
dead-end job, 67
decision making, 62
decision-making power, 65, 68
declined, 5
declining, 2, 15, 39, 47
declining spending, 16
Delaware, 14
demand, 4, 54, 56–57, 129, 131–32
demographic outlook, 4–6
demographic shifts, 2, 7, 111
demographic transformations, 1, 7
deniers archetype, 52–54
deportation threats, 81, 111
D&I (diversity and inclusion), 103, 105–7, 110, 112, 119–20, 136
differences, 4, 8, 27, 42, 46, 72, 87, 95–96, 124, 130, 138
  cultural-dynamics, 46
D&I mastery, 112
disciplined, 141, 150
Dish, 57
disrupter, 147
disruptive, xvii, 43, 111
dissolution, 69
distractors, 45, 100
distribution channels, 8, 94
District of Columbia, 13–14
diverse communities, 80
diverse consumers, 33, 105, 119
diverse cultural group, 87
diverse population, xii, 62, 91, 111
diverse staffing needs, 105

diversity, 100–103, 106–7, 109–12, 119, 131, 137
  ethnic, 102, 110
diversity councils, 107
diversity-hire goals, 107
Diversity Inc., 112
divestitures, 39
divisions, 27, 63, 75, 85, 120, 148
DIY behavior, 28–29
double-digit growth, 24
dreamers, 81, 104, 106, 111, 119, 137
drive-by, 56
duality, 3
due diligence, 44, 46, 57, 143
due-diligence analysis, 58, 69
dynamic, 22, 67, 95
dynamics, xi, 23, 28, 46, 62, 88, 147

E

earnings report, 22
EBIT (earnings before interest and taxes), 102
EBITDA (earnings before interest, taxes, depreciation, and amortization), 38
economically viable, 9, 39
economic benefits, xii
economic boom, 5
economic clout, 7
economic foundations, 6
economic indicators, 41
economic outlooks, 41
economic potential, 90, 113
economic powerhouse, 21
economy, xi, 11, 22, 81
education, 11, 31, 35–36, 41, 46, 136
elementary level, xiv, 58
El Pollo Loco, 69
embrace, 3, 8, 15, 84, 122
emerging market, 21–22, 40
employee development, 109

integration, xiv, 38, 62, 67–68, 72–73, 122, 127

integrity, 39, 71, 93–95, 97, 99

intellectual capital, 143–44

interdependencies, 118

intermittent, xiv

Internal analyses, 28

internal competition, 146–47

internal experts, 68, 140

internal indifference, 73

internal resistance, 29

internal resistance to change, 78

internal teams, 63

internal traction, 142, 147

international expansion, ix, 21

international markets, 21, 56

international sales, 22

intrapreneurial mind-set, 45

investment, ix–x, xiii, 21, 25, 40, 43, 48, 52, 65, 75, 77, 79, 96, 118, 125, 131, 145–47

investors, 22

irrelevant, xiii, 49, 53, 73, 142

irrelevant resource allocation, 73

IT (information technology), 129

J

job growth, 13

Johnson & Johnson, 56, 112

Jung, Carl, 51

junior brand associate, 55, 62, 65

K

Kilts, Jim, 54, 148

Korean, 11

KPIs (key performance indicators), 25–26, 45, 57, 63–64, 72, 102, 138

Kraft Foods, 148–49, 160

Kranc, Lisa, xvii, 28–29

Kroger Co., xvii, 26, 48

L

labor force participation, 32

labor shortage, 4

labor vacuum, 4

leadership involvement, 46, 63, 150

leadership oversight, 45

leadership team, 75, 120, 147–48

learning curves, 40

life expectancy, 18

life stages, 15

lifetime value advantage, 15

lifetime value potential, 15

long-term economic impact, 22

long-term implications, 53

long-term strategies, 74–75

long-term thinkers, 122

L'Oréal, 22

Louisiana, 14

low-key, 43

loyalty, 39

loyalty data, 29

M

major appliances, 23

majority minority population, 7, 83

majority non-white, 1

majority population, 1

management, 13, 24, 44, 48, 64, 77, 97–98, 109, 114, 133, 136, 144, 146

management models, 73

mandatory, 50

manifestation, cultural, 8

market advantage, 39

market characteristics, 30

market dominance, xi

market expansion, 75, 147

market-immersion experiences, 88

marketing, x, xvii, 27–28, 30, 48–49, 59, 61, 63, 66, 72–73, 82, 98,

Printed in the United States
by Bo

Printed in the United States
By Bookmasters